I0491564

Thank you to my wonderful husband

and best friend for always supporting and encouraging me.

Also, to my incredibly special children,

for the joy and inspiration you continually bring me.

Thanks to my Dad for his wisdom and encouragement.

And most importantly to God for my faith.

Contents

Foreword

Leading a successful business is challenging and requires numerous skill sets, as anyone who has tried can attest. But one of the areas of leadership that has not been focused upon enough is *implementation*. An organization can have a great product or service, a solid marketing plan, and knowledgeable, talented team members. But if, together, they aren't able to "get the job done", all of their planning and efforts go to waste.

In *It's All about the How*, Teri Giannetti provides a thorough, structured approach to help leaders move from initial ideas to successfully delivering their products to their customers. Whether you are an experienced or beginning leader, or someone who aspires to become a leader, this book will help you move forward in your professional development.

Drawing from her years of experience as an executive and consultant in the banking and financial services industries, Teri provides practical, real life examples to demonstrate how to utilize the numerous tools and resources she provides. Her theme of "talk and plan less, do more, and do it well" is consistent throughout the book and provides a solid foundation to getting tasks done (from personal improvement to large scale system change). By reading and applying the principles Teri gives, you will learn "all about the how" and be able to lead others in executing the business plans that will make your company successful.

Paul White, Ph.D.
Psychologist
Co-author, *The 5 Languages of Appreciation in the Workplace*
Author, *The Vibrant Workplace*

Well done

is better than

well said.

— Benjamin Franklin

CHAPTER 1

Why Focus on the "How"?

"Well done is better than well said."
— Benjamin Franklin

I have had a graveyard of corporate binders on my shelves. They represented countless hours of planning strategic initiatives that often amounted to little in terms of business results. Perhaps your shelf has a row of binders, too. If you don't have old binders, then maybe you have a few large presentations in your email archives from strategic planning sessions of previous years.

Smart business leaders typically spend enormous amounts of time and money developing (and redeveloping) new strategies full of promising ideas. But management turnover and short-sighted focus on quarterly results leaves these well-crafted strategies in old dusty binders taking up shelf space—literally or virtually.

How many of the ideas in these binders and plans were well executed? How many of them were never executed at all? Have new plans already replaced the old ones? I've seen initiatives deployed unsuccessfully five years ago that were relaunched by new leaders who were unaware of past failures. One author suggests that up to 90 percent of business strategies fail due to poor execution and failed implementation (Keyte, 2012). I've seen this proven in my own twenty-year business career.

I have spent a large portion of my time in business developing and implementing strategic initiatives. What have I learned that would help others? The single most important lesson I learned throughout my journey, hands down, is that successful strategies depend on the quality of the

"How." As Benjamin Franklin once stated, "Well done is better than well said." That's what this book is designed to help you with. Talk and plan less; do more, and do it well.

I've seen brilliant initiatives abandoned due to failed execution. Sometimes this occurs due to leadership changes. As a participant and leader in many strategic planning discussions, I've often reminded colleagues to not get caught up in the details of the "What" because the success of the effort will be determined by the quality of implementation—the "How." So, enough of the strategy discussions.

This book will examine the key components necessary to successfully *implement* your strategies. The book will focus on how to quickly determine a valid strategy, how to leverage proven tools to develop an implementation P.L.A.N., how to gain leadership support, how to effectively communicate, and, finally, how to monitor project implementation for success.

Have you ever experienced a well-defined strategy that fell apart during execution? I have and it was almost always due to poor attention to the details of implementation. Paying attention to details can seem less important, but the details of implementation are the key to success.

Talk and plan less; do more, and do it well.

Any NBA coach will tell you that game strategy is important, but they'll also tell you that winning takes great players who execute on the court. Likewise, companies that have been very successful over the long-term, such as Toyota or Google, have maintained consistent strategies and have focused more on flawless execution.

Netflix is a good example of a company that had the right strategy but completely failed upon execution. The company first launched its video-streaming business, then titled "Quickster," as a separate brand. They split the company, which not only made the business more complicated for customers, but also caused a 60 percent price increase for customers who wanted both services. Existing customers weren't grandfathered into the new price structure at the old rate, causing serious negativity and general confusion.

According to CNET, the poor execution by Netflix cost the company tremendously. Netflix lost eight hundred thousand subscribers and its stock price dropped 77 percent in just four months (Sandoval, 2012).

As we can see with the Netflix example, the cost of poorly executed strategies can be huge. We also see a tremendous number of small businesses fail for the same reason. *Inc.* magazine reported in 2015 that 96 percent of small businesses fail within ten years (Carmody, 2015). Do businesses fail because they have a bad strategy? Possibly, but in most cases the idea is good; it's the execution, the "How," that fell short.

The principle of focusing on the "How" over the "What" also applies outside of business. Just look at underdogs. Here are two examples, one from the world of soccer, and another about an ancient story of a Good Samaritan.

Almost everyone loves the story of the underdog. Have you ever stopped to wonder why people cheer for the underdog and gain so much pleasure when they win? It's because underdogs have the lesser "What" in relation to skill levels, experience, knowledge, and financial resources. The underdog is humbler and more endearing because they know they are not likely to win. Their chances of winning are slim and so they are forced to rely heavily on better execution, the "How" of playing the game.

In sports, the "How" includes qualities such as having more endurance, running faster, or having more desire to win than an opponent. In other words, the underdog has to work harder at executing the fundamentals. When they are able to overcome a stronger opponent, it's usually because of a maniacal focus on the "How."

One of the most incredible underdog stories I have ever heard is the 2016 Leicester City soccer team's championship win in England's Premier League, one of the world's most elite professional soccer leagues. Leicester City had never won the Premier League championship and the odds against them winning during the 2015-2016 season were five thousand to one. Their season started with a new, seasoned coach, Claudio Ranieri. Claudio was an Italian player and professional soccer coach with a long career of producing successful teams. Before he took over, the Leicester City team had finished the previous season in fourteenth place. Although they had a billionaire owner, their budget was significantly less than other teams within the Premier League.

So, how did they achieve such an amazing feat against all odds? During the season, Leicester City did far from the best in terms of possession or passing, but they did very well on defense. More importantly, several commentators noticed that they had *great spirit*. Many, if not most, successful underdogs share this trait. They simply have more desire to win than the opponent.

In the case of Leicester City, they had a *simple strategy* to win. They started the season with less "What" in terms of record, budget, and overall passing and possession skills. But they were able to achieve the unimaginable through amazing defensive execution and strong spirit to win.

Next, consider the old, but familiar story of the "Good Samaritan." In the context of this Biblical story, the Samaritans were considered unclean by the Jewish teachers to whom Jesus was speaking when he told this story. In fact, the individual who asked Jesus to define "neighbor" was considered to be an expert in the law. Jesus answered by sharing the parable of the Good Samaritan.

In the story, a foreigner is attacked by robbers, stripped, beaten, and left lying on the side of the road. Two highly regarded religious individuals both see the wounded man, but do nothing to help him. A third man, a lowly Samaritan, comes along. Because he is a Samaritan, he is considered by the elite crowd as someone unworthy, an outcast. But it is the Samaritan who has pity on the injured man and ultimately helps him.

Jesus then asks the expert in the law, which, of the three men, was the true neighbor to the wounded man on the side of the road. The answer, of course was the one who had mercy on the foreigner. Therefore, the Samaritan was ultimately recognized not for having an elite heritage, but for the "How," the way he *acted* to help the man (Luke 10:25-37, New International Version).

In both examples, we see that how something is done is what makes the difference.

Shift your attention back to business and look at another example in a small manufacturing company. The company had an average strategy, but focused on improving execution with the help of a successful manufacturing consultant. The consultant also happened to be my father, and he had more than twenty years of experience working with several of the nation's leading corporations, government agencies and small companies. He is also a Lean instructor and applies these philosophies to produce results in companies of all sizes.

In both examples, we see that how something is done is what makes the difference.

He helped this small manufacturer quickly assess what they needed to improve and they decided to focus on their procurement efforts. This process rep-resented a significant portion of their cost-of-goods sold. They leveraged a common Lean tool called "value stream mapping" to diagram all of the activities of the procurement department to pinpoint waste.

They mapped the process, established a cross-functional team to ensure engagement, and focused on executing a simple strategy to eliminate all non-value-added activities. This way their buyers could concentrate on working with the suppliers as "partners" versus "adversaries." The process educated many on the team and provided the level of engagement needed to ensure that non-value-added activities would be eliminated.

The effort maintained strong engagement and was well executed and celebrated. It also saved the company almost $50,000 in non-value-added activities in the first year alone. The intangible benefit was a new attitude. The team was now focused on continuous improvement by leveraging the methodology. They sought to identify other non-value-added processes within the company. The keys to success included a defined and simple strategy, early engagement by a cross-functional team, and a strong focus on implementation.

These examples, while distinct in nature, emphasize the importance of how to execute a plan or strategy. Therefore, no matter what size business you are a part of, and regardless of your role, this book will provide a fresh and comprehensive look at the importance of elevating the "How" when you develop or execute your next brilliant strategy. It will also provide you with practical tools to ensure success.

The following chapters include the crucial components of a successful implementation, such as: quickly determining a valid strategy; leveraging proven tools to develop an execution P.L.A.N.; gaining vital leadership support; developing effective communications; and monitoring progress for success. Once you master and implement these concepts, you will see results and agree that in the end, *it's all about the how.*

If you want to win,

when it comes to strategy,

ponder less and do more.

— Jack Welch, *Winning*

CHAPTER 2

Efficiently Define the "What"

Have you ever been a part of a planning effort that took so long it never got off the ground? I have. It was painful to expend so much energy on an initiative that was never realized. Sadly, this happens all the time in business.

We have to acknowledge that the world is constantly evolving. The pace of change keeps increasing exponentially. This means that leaders and managers need to develop quality strategies quickly. Being too slow to deliver on an idea or initiative can significantly impact the overall success. We can see some examples of this within the technology industry. Product launch timing is critical, and delivering a quality product too late can result in significant revenue losses. For example, think about the booming tablet market. The tablet concept was originally developed in 2005 by Microsoft, not Apple. While Microsoft was still working on *the idea,* Apple launched one of the most successful products of all time—the iPad—in 2010.

This chapter will provide you with useful insights and tools on how to define a high quality "What" (strategy) as quickly and efficiently as possible. This involves assembling the right team, building consensus for the strategy, and developing a project charter to guide the effort. We will look more closely at each of these three elements in this chapter.

First, it's important to be clear about what the "What" means. The "What" is the business strategy. As a manager of strategic initiatives for many years, I know that the most effective strategies succinctly define the direction of an organization or line of business over a specific time frame. The *concept* of the "What" should be simple and clear.

Second, the best strategies are crafted so that they are *simple to execute*. It can be easy to forget that companies are made up of people, and people are limited by the number of efforts they can deliver at the same time. I've seen strategies designed in ways that are so complex that teams struggle to understand them, let alone implement them. I guarantee that if employees can't understand a strategy, then they will not be able to execute it.

With these two factors in mind, let's look at how to develop the "What," or strategy, quickly and efficiently. It doesn't matter if your role is a change manager or a business executive, the next three steps will help you accomplish the task.

1. Assembling the Right Team

Imagine that your boss has delivered the exciting news that she would like you to solve the company's most pressing business challenge: low customer-satisfaction results. The good news is that she has confidence in you to lead the effort to improve the situation. The bad news is that it will be a huge challenge to implement a plan that will actually improve customer satisfaction.

The best strategies are crafted so that they are *simple to execute*.

Therefore, depending on the size of your organization, your first task will usually be to *assemble a cross-functional team of experts*. There are likely many employees, including managers and frontline staff, who know the reasons for poor customer feedback and the right approach to fixing the problems. I've often said to my teams that the solutions to problems can almost always be identified best by the people who do the work. For this reason, the cross-functional team should include front-line staff, the people "on the ground" who know first-hand what is happening.

Depending on the topic and size of the business, the cross-functional team should also comprise employees from various disciplines, including IT, marketing, sales, product development, operations, compliance, HR, and communications. Since crafting strategies is typically perceived as glamorous work, members of this team often feel honored to be included in such efforts. Your task will be to ensure you have involved the appropriate groups and stakeholders and then to use their time wisely in the mission of crafting the right strategy—as fast as you possibly can.

Once the right individuals are identified, the next step is to build strong team relationships. The best approach will depend on several factors, including the complexity of the initiative, how well the team members already know each other, and time and cost considerations.

After you assess your situation, you will need to decide if the team will meet face-to-face, virtually, or some combination of both. Typically, if the team is new and participants don't know one another, face-to-face meetings are best, at least initially. Nothing will help a team connect better than time spent getting to know each other personally and professionally. Planning team-building events are ideal for helping people connect personally, if the budget allows. Even if teams have worked together for some time, holding a periodic team event, perhaps quarterly, helps ensure team cohesiveness. The most successful teams I've experienced have had the luxury to meet weekly, or at least quarterly.

Many times, face-to-face team development is not possible. In these cases, especially if teams have successfully worked with each other in the past, and the initiative is relatively straightforward, team connections can be managed virtually.

Regardless of the approach, the key is to build relationships and trust, to be able to leverage expertise so that you can quickly define a high-quality and simple "What."

Another key factor in building the right cross-functional team is the effectiveness of meetings. We will examine face-to-face and virtual meetings. If you have the time and funding to bring a team together in person, then holding the meetings off-site will typically shorten the time needed to gain the team's consensus.

The best structure for effective face-to-face off-site meetings is for the leader to invest time upfront in careful planning, so that the group can easily stay on task during the meeting. A poorly executed off-site meeting will not be fruitful. It will waste the time of the participants and yours. Also, an ineffective off-site meeting will set a negative tone for the effort, which can discourage the future engagement and support of the participants and key stakeholders.

I have participated in countless off-site meetings and one stood out as an example of what can go wrong in an inefficient meeting. It was designed to address an annual sales force incentive plan. For starters, the meeting lacked structure. Although it included a cross-functional team, there was a loose agenda, and there were too many participants for the meeting to be effective. Admittedly, developing incentive plans is always hotly debated in sales organizations. There are many competing voices from management, product areas, finance, risk, and operations. This situation was no different, with a broad cross-functional team that had already been meeting for several months. Unfortunately, despite hours and hours of meetings, the group had not been able to arrive at a consensus, and time was running out.

The leader of the business finally stepped in, demanded that the team meet in-person for four days to finalize the plan. Those were some of the longest days in my career up to that point. Grueling conversations occurred over breakfast, lunch, and dinner in the same room. The result? Well, in my opinion, the team's plan turned out to be overly complicated. Because of all the competing priorities, the final plan tried to appease everyone, and that made it incredibly complicated to execute with the sales teams. Trying to craft a perfect "What" that fulfills every management edict in the company will almost always fail. The strategy will become so complicated that employees won't be able to figure it out, and it will lack the flexibility needed to handle unforeseen circumstances.

You may notice from this example that the team spent extensive time talking and thinking about the "What." Had this group focused on the "How," they could have saved dozens of hours. They would have been better off working on ways to *implement* the prior year's plan than to use so much time and talent on developing a new strategy.

These same team-building principles also apply in relation to virtual meetings. Today, many meetings are held virtually. They offer the advantage of reduced travel time and lower travel costs. Although many of the same off-site meeting rules apply to virtual meetings, there are some important nuances to consider that will ensure effectiveness. Thankfully, technology offers many tools to foster your success.

Whenever possible, the best virtual meeting option is to use programs that allow participants to see each other. If everyone has access to the Internet, this should be easy to accomplish. There are many free tools, such as Google Hangouts, Skype, join.me, Zoom, etc. These will help ensure that multi-tasking among the participants is limited, and it helps to build relationships.

However, if technological constraints allow for audio-only conference calls, the leader should apply the same meeting management principles as in other types of meetings. Strategies to minimize interruptions and multi-tasking will also be important. At the start of a virtual meeting, make sure that everyone understands the expectations and goals. Ask everyone to place all microphones on mute when not in use. Use chat functions so that participants can ask and respond to questions. Advise members about the timeline and agenda of the meeting. Make sure that presenters communicate clearly and enthusiastically. That will keep folks engaged and minimize multitasking.

With the right expectations and leadership, virtual teams can be highly effective.

Building a Consensus

Once you have the right team and are running effective meetings, you will need to build a consensus for your strategy. This starts with effective planning so that you can lead a discussion that will produce results. Unfortunately, many managers and leaders are dealing with fewer and fewer resources, which infringes on the time they need to plan. As a result, many feel tempted to skip the planning. Leaders must resist this temptation and make sure that careful thought is put into planning the event.

By far the most fruitful approach to gaining consensus is to follow carefully crafted meeting agendas with the specific objectives in mind. In one such effort I led, I knew the group of high-level employees would have only eight hours to agree upon a plan for a strategic initiative. The business challenge was to design a strategy to deepen client relationships with limited human resources. This business was requesting a new approach to customer segmentation.

After careful preparation and early consultation with key stakeholders, I led the off-site meeting by outlining the project charter, providing a well-defined problem statement, clarifying our objectives, and asking good questions for the group to answer. Each question was developed with potential alternatives for the group to consider. (It's easier for people to react to alternatives than to brainstorm.) We also had a strict timeline during the day, and we stuck to it. By the end of the day the team had agreed on a solid initial approach. This would be presented to senior leaders for approval.

We then spent the next eighteen months *executing* the new client segmentation strategy. It was widely adopted and very successful, in large part because we obtained expert input from the cross-functional team and quickly reached a consensus for our strategy. By defining the "What" speedily and decisively, would could give all our attention to the "How," or, in other words, effective execution.

A common pitfall when attempting to gain a consensus is allowing for too much collaboration. Collaboration is an awesome problem solving approach because it brings together different voices that often develop more complete or better solutions. Although as we see in the incentive planning team example above, having too many competing voices can sabotage an effort.

Collaboration can slow progress down as everyone seeks a compromise. For example, sales managers will typically want to keep their goals lower, to ensure they are attainable. This may conflict with the goals of finance managers, who want higher sales goals because they are being pushed to come up with double-digit revenue growth. A customer service manager may want to ensure the right products and services are sold, rather than just those that will achieve the most revenue, since they will have to deal with unhappy customers.

The point is, trying to please everyone will be impossible, and it will hinder decision-making. The business will need to decide which measures are the most critical to track based on their strategy. Supporting this fact is Deloitte's CFO Signals™ survey published quarterly, which suggested that the problem of differing views and competing goals was a primary barrier to making decisions (Deloitte LLP, 2012).

Developing a Project Charter

The next element of efficiently developing a strategy is to *outline the business case for the effort.* Basically, this means creating a well-developed project charter. Project charters are based on input from senior leaders, your own knowledge, and other subject-matter experts. Although many tools exist to assist in communicating the business case for an initiative, I'm a fan of the Six Sigma project charter formats. These are simple to use and provide a good structure to ensure you have captured all necessary components for a strategic initiative.

A typical project charter for the Six Sigma "Define" phase will include some or all of the following elements, as shown in the sample image on the next page.

The next element of efficiently developing a strategy is to *outline the business case for the effort.*

Problem Statement: Defines the problem and quantifies the value of the opportunity in solving it. The problem statement does not state the solution. A simple example of a problem statement could be something like this: "The current model is insufficient to produce desired revenue goals."

Business Case & Benefits: Describes the rationale for the effort, including a definition of the "What" that is to be accomplished, such as to increase revenue growth by the better alignment of sales resources to opportunities, including investment in hiring where needed.

Scope: Identifies the boundaries of the initiative, typically defining "in-scope" and "out-of-scope." For example, customer safety may be in-scope, whereas employee safety could be out-of-scope.

Created by: _____
Date Updated: _____

DEFINE

Project Charter "Process Name"

Problem Statement

Quantify what is broken.
The current cycle time of 41 days to deliver Product ABC after order completion does not meet customers expectations and is impacting overall customer satisfaction ratings. Reducing the delivery time should improve customer satisfaction ratings by X % while maintaining quality standards.

Business Case & Benefits

Best estimate of financial benefits Finance/accounting signoff on verifiability.
This project was initiated to fix the problem of long cycle times to deliver Product ABC. One of the items on the business balanced scorecard is to improve this performance. If this project is not undertaken, then we could potentially lose a major customer resulting in a potential revenue loss of $1MM.

Goal Statement

Succinct statement of what measures will be impacted? By how much? By when?
The goal of this project is to reduce cycle time for delivery of Product ABC from 41 days to 15 days by project completion date.

Primary & Secondary Metrics

Primary	Secondary
Product delivery cycle time	Product Quality
Revenue	

Scope In/Out & Key Risks

Define project boundaries and risks.
In-Scope: Product ABC
Out of Scope: All other products
Key Risk: Reducing cycle time to del... prod... ABC could adversely effect quality. Need to ensure existing quality standards maintained with new process.

Project Team & Key Stakeholders

Name	Department
J... ..S..th	Product Marketing
A... rea... on ;	Accounting
S... ...rt	Sales
B... Loot	Customer Service

Customer Critical to Quality (CTQ)

Product ABC delivered within 15 days after order completion.

Timeline

Key Milestone	Target
Start Date	
DMAIC Tollgates	
Completion Date	

Rationale & Key Risks: Outlines why the strategy is important, describes the key risks, and, suggests areas that may impede the success of the initiative. In the example above, reducing cycle time to deliver the product could reduce quality.

Goal Statement / Financial Benefits (also referred to as the cost of poor quality): Quantifies the value of expected improvements based on successful implementation of the objective. If incremental revenue growth is the key objective, the benefit section would quantify how much revenue the initiative would likely generate in the current fiscal year, or in future years.

Process: Describes the process to be reviewed and improved upon. In some instances, when a project is new, the process may not yet exist. If that is the case, the project charter should note that the process is still-to-be defined. In an example of increasing the sales rate of a certain product, the pipeline process could be well-defined.

Customer Critical to Quality (CTQ) Attributes: Outlines the elements that are critical to the customer, based on input from customers.

Project Team Members, Stakeholders and End-Users: Outlines key participants in the project and their role as subject-matter experts, the necessary stakeholders for approving the initiative, and the end-users who will ultimately be impacted by the changes.

Primary and Secondary Metrics: Defines the key measures that will be used to assess progress. The primary metric is referenced throughout the project as a measure of success, such as client satisfaction. The secondary metric is a countermeasure to ensure that the primary metric is not causing the secondary metric to decrease. For example, if product quality is our secondary measure, we want to make sure that does not go down when we make changes elsewhere.

Timeline: Outlines how long the project is expected to take and the key milestones throughout the process.

The key is to provide a thoughtful basis for the project team to work from that will be impactful to the business. A well-prepared project charter will provide the team with a framework that allows for focusing on the "How."

The initial project charter doesn't need to be 100 percent complete before the first discussion with the team; in fact, I would recommend having the team work together to finalize key components of the plan for adoption purposes. The more ownership of the plan you can instill in your team, the better your adoption and execution will be. Regardless, as the project leader, you should still draft the project charter prior to the first discussion. As you do this, focus on the business case, the problem statement, the scope, and the project goals and timelines to provide the group with a clear starting point.

The team can then work on refining the project charter together, setting realistic timeframes, determining the best ways to measure success, establishing parameters for the scope of the effort, and deciding if additional stakeholders should be involved. If you've assembled the right team of stakeholders and they agree on the strategy and plan to execute, then the execution will be simpler.

> **A well-prepared project charter will provide the team with a framework that allows for focusing on the "How."**

Conclusion

Once you have 1) gained consensus on the strategy; 2) assembled the right team to lead the execution; and 3) finalized the initial project charter, you are ready to develop the "How." The next chapter outlines my practical approach for developing your "How" P.L.A.N. so that you can successfully deliver results when so many others before you have failed.

Execution starts with focus.

—McChesney, Covey & Huling
The 4 Disciplines of Execution

CHAPTER 3

Creating Your "How" P.L.A.N.

N ow that you have determined the "What," we will turn to the main purpose of this book, which is about reinforcing the *importance* of the "How" and providing you with *a simple approach* for executing your strategy.

Although we sometimes feel overloaded with acronyms, the reality is that good ones help us remember the most important elements of the initiatives they represent. That's why I developed the following "How" P.L.A.N. It's simple to remember and, based on my experience, it contains the key elements to effectively implement change. The acronym includes the following:

> **P** = Planning how to execute
>
> **L** = Leadership support
>
> **A** = Adoption within a group
>
> **N** = Need to monitor and control

Applying the P.L.A.N. approach when developing the "How" will help ensure successful execution. For example, if we look at Toyota's incredible success through the P.L.A.N. lens, we see that they have a well-defined plan that is focused on delivering the highest quality product. Toyota's leaders support the "How" by fostering an atmosphere of continuous improvement. The percentage of employees who adopt the plan is high, and the majority of the company's employees are engaged and offering suggestions for improvement throughout the year. Finally, the company has leveraged a definitive system to measure quality that helps them monitor and control the outcomes. So, if you want to enjoy some of Toyota's success, keep reading. We will look at each of these components in more detail, starting with "Planning."

P = Planning How to Execute

Within the "How" P.L.A.N., P stands for planning, which is about how to execute. This is simple, but not easy. Barriers to planning include limited resources and time constraints. Although taking time to plan can feel like a luxury, it is critical to successful implementation.

A good technique to help this step move faster is to ask yourself and your team members some important questions. The answers to these questions will produce the tactics you will deploy in your execution. Sample questions to consider are:

1) Which employees will be impacted and how?
2) Who needs to be involved?
3) Will it change what they are doing today?
4) Do systems support your change?
5) Do employees have capacity to change?
6) How will they feel about the change?
7) Who will lead the change?
8) Will customers or suppliers be impacted?
9) How will they feel about the change?
10) How will you measure success?

It is common for teams to avoid fully considering these questions. For example, imagine that you are implementing a process-improvement effort that will save time for those working in operations by automating the steps earlier in the process. The automation enhancement, however, will *add* work to those who are completing the steps before those who are working in operations. And those people are already overworked. Thus, the expected gains in efficiency from the operational team will be overshadowed by setbacks in other areas.

The point is this: If leaders fail to consider the impact of changes on *all* employees (see question 1 above), then implementation will be hindered. Therefore, it is important to take the time to think through these questions. Doing so will significantly increase your success rate.

A question that is often dismissed is number six, regarding feelings. Employees are people and people have feelings. Sure, employees are paid to do their jobs, but how they feel about the job matters. Using the example above, the group that had to take on more work although they were already overworked, did not feel good about the changes. When employees have negative feelings about changes, they will most likely lack motivation, which can significantly hinder execution.

In addition to this simple list of questions, the Six Sigma toolbox can help you think through all aspects of implementation. That is why I've included an overview of how to leverage popular Six Sigma tools to develop your "How" in the next chapter.

L = Leadership Support

Have you ever had a bad manager or leader? If so, how motivated were you to do the tasks they required of you? Most of us have worked for ineffective managers or leaders at various points in our careers. When I assumed leadership for a new team, I would frequently say that "leadership matters," because it does. When it comes to executing your "How," you will absolutely need leadership support to be successful. I've seen brilliant strategies never executed because leaders did not support the plan, or because they were ineffective in motivating the team to change. Quality people can easily be demotivated and produce bad results when led by an ineffective manager.

Quality people can easily be demotivated and produce bad results when led by an ineffective manager.

A great example can be found in sports. Most winning teams have amazing coaches that provide the leadership needed to help the team achieve greatness. The strongest leaders adjust their style to the individual they are motivating. These leaders often make up for a lack of experience or talent by using interpersonal skills. This is what the coaches of the "less-talented" Leicester City soccer team did when they won England's Premier League championship in 2016. The same principle holds true in business. Leadership is required to be successful, especially over the long-term.

I was once a part of a national strategic effort that brilliantly married qualitative and quantitative data to identify revenue growth opportunities within a mature line of business. For several years, the effort had a well-defined "How" plan, executive leadership support, strong adoption among employees, and a good monitoring system. However, after a few years the executive leadership changed and the new leaders did not support the effort. Therefore, despite still having the other three components in place, the effort quickly was abandoned.

At the end of the day, leadership support is the most important element that drives change.

At the end of the day, leadership support is the most important element that drives change. Without it, your effort is almost guaranteed to fail. Much research has been done that suggests a lack of leadership is one of the top reasons efforts fail. I would agree.

Identifying Key Leaders

How do you know if you have the support of all impacted leaders? If you don't know the answer to that question, then I'd suggest after you finish reading this chapter, you review your notes to ensure you have all appropriate support. Depending on the size of your organization and the authority structure, this could include executives, mid-level, and front-line managers of the group that will be impacted by the change.

Typically, key decision-makers and stakeholders are individuals with direct responsibility for the teams who will implement the initiative. In larger organizations with a matrix management system, leaders or managers with dotted-line authority over a specific program could also be key decision-makers. Within this context, you still may not know all the leaders. So, step one is to ask the known leaders if they recommend any other individuals who should be involved in the planning phases. Although this step seems straight forward, it's often overlooked. When key leaders are inadvertently excluded, projects can stall because important viewpoints and talents have not been included.

Let's imagine that a marketing department decides to run a promotion to increase sales volume. After many months of planning the promotions, developing materials, outlining incentives, and communicating with the sales force, the head of marketing decides to inform the head of customer service about the project just before it's scheduled to be launched. The customer service manager is concerned because the project will likely increase call volume at a time when the department is understaffed due to layoffs. Suddenly, the marketing leaders realize that a key stakeholder has been excluded. The reality is that the customer service manager is a key stakeholder in this effort. Had she been contacted early in the process, the company might have been able to avoid layoffs. At a minimum, she could have informed the marketing director that her department would not be able to handle the additional calls. Now poor leadership engagement has created a crisis, and the entire effort might be postponed or abandoned. This example demonstrates that it's worth the effort and time to identify and contact all pertinent decision-makers and leaders.

How to Gain Leadership Support

Based on my experiences with leading strategic initiatives, most leaders like to see a draft of the plan that outlines the problem statement and the project's value to the business. The Six Sigma project charter (see Chapter 2) provides a nice template to ensure you have outlined the necessary components to present to stakeholders as you seek their support.

The following real-world example shows how lack of leadership support can cause a one-hundred-year-old company to go out of business. Gary Kerslake, a forty-year veteran in manufacturing, worked for many years with a company that built high-quality diesel engines. The company had a high rate of on-time delivery, and at one point, the company controlled 70 percent of the market.

Then energy scarcity emerged as a national economic issue. Customers began to ask the company to reduce the weight of the engine while increasing fuel efficiency and horsepower. Unfortunately, the large egos of key leaders and engineers got in the way of common sense. Customers were asking for lighter weight and more efficient machines, but the product engineers could not be persuaded to change. They felt they had the best engine designs in the world, and that was that. At product review meetings, they made comments such as, "What does the customer really know about engine design?" and, "We have the best engine in the world! Just look at our market share."

Unfortunately, the company's market share slowly eroded every year due to a lack of leadership support for plans to re-engineer designs. Within ten years, the company was completely out of the diesel engine business and it eventually went totally out of business.

Clearly, adjusting the design was critical to future sales based on environmental factors and customer desires, but leadership support didn't materialize. As a result, this company paid the ultimate price (going out of business). Had the business case been presented more effectively, leadership support for design updates could have been achieved! Had that occurred, this company might still be in business today.

Let's look next at the third letter in the "How" P.L.A.N., which is about gaining employee support for your effort.

A = Adoption within a Group

Have you ever been a part of team that didn't work well together? Have you heard the complaints of fellow employees who were not happy about a new process or system? Have you been one of those employees? If so, the problem is rooted in poor employee adoption of a strategy, which is the "A" within P.L.A.N.

Change managers might have a great plan and solid leadership support, but without employee adoption, initiatives still fail. The good news is there are many ways to gain employee adoption once you have leadership support. Based on my experience, it is more effective to use several of the following approaches.

The first method is to engage employees in the planning phase. I firmly believe that employees doing the work have the answers to all problems within a business. This is a basic premise of Lean and Six Sigma; the best individuals to identify opportunities and to improve a process are those who currently execute the process. Therefore, by soliciting employee feedback about an initiative and by applying it to your end solution, you will not only garner support from employees, but you will also likely get a better solution.

I once heard about a small machine shop that kept trying to improve its product quality without engaging the company's machinists. The managers were frustrated by lackluster results from changes they insisted on making without input from the employees working the machines. The machinists could have told them they were not addressing the core problem, which was vibration in the machines.

Change managers might have a great plan and solid leadership support, but without employee adoption, initiatives still fail.

Instead, they kept adjusting the process, which wasted time and resources, and frustrated the employees who were never consulted.

By contrast, Toyota is a company that has throughout its history worked hard to engage employees early in change processes. It's said that Toyota receives an average of nine ideas per employee per year. With more than three-hundred-thousand employees, that's an impressive 2.7 million suggestions per year (Power, 2011)! The power of Toyota's approach is reflected in their high-quality product and significant revenue results.

As you use this approach, you should ensure that you communicate with your employees about the value of their feedback, and celebrate the positive impact they have had on the process of achieving a strong outcome. This will help with building team rapport, and ensure better and faster adoption of the plan. (We will discuss communication efforts in more detail in Chapter 5.)

Another method of improving employee adoption of plans is to establish employee champions who assist with the transition to the new program or initiative. The champions not only serve as experts on the new initiative, but they are also a resource to gather feedback to be shared with managers and leaders. The reality is that change is hard for most individuals. Sticking with what we know and doing things the way we have always done them seems easier. Therefore, assigning a champion to serve as a role model and mentor will provide support to teams as they go through very normal phases of resistance to change. A side benefit of assigning champions is that it gives employees a chance to lead others and to grow in their professional abilities.

It's best to select your top performing individuals as champions and then give them what they need to effectively serve in this capacity. If executed correctly, this approach will improve the team's sincere adoption of the initiative. This approach also provides individual development opportunities for those selected to be champions.

The reality is that change is hard for most individuals.

Another approach to employee engagement is to offer employee recognition and incentives throughout the transition process. As mentioned, change is hard for most people. Incentives can help them adopt new behaviors. Most people are motivated by rewards, although the right incentive varies from person to person.

To be effective at employee recognition, you must study your team and understand what motivates them personally. A great resource on effective recognition efforts can be found in the book, *The 5 Languages of Appreciation in the Workplace,* written by Dr. Gary Chapman and Dr. Paul White. These authors state that overall job satisfaction among employees depends most on recognition. ". . . the number one factor in job satisfaction is not the amount of pay but whether or not the individual feels appreciated and valued for the work they do," write Chapman and White (p. 15). I agree with this statement wholeheartedly. I have used their model while managing a large sales team and while helping to implement more effective recognition programs.

Although we will discuss this topic more in Chapter 5, as it pertains to effective communications, the premise of Chapman and White's book is simply that individuals tend to feel appreciated most in one or two of the following five categories:

Words of Affirmation: This is the language that uses words to communicate a positive message to another person. According to the book, this involves verbally affirming a positive characteristic about a person (p. 46). An example might be to publicly praise the person for a job well done.

Quality Time: This is the act of giving an individual dedicated, focused attention (p. 59). A good way to appreciate these individuals is for the manager to set up weekly meetings and to give full attention to the employee during those times.

Acts of Service: This type of individual feels most appreciated when they are offered assistance. You can show appreciation by offering to help them with a task and then following through on the commitment. An example is to help them complete administrative work or get a presentation completed in time. Chapman and White share a story about a team of leaders at a small business that needed to complete an important presentation by the next day. The team, including the president of the company, stayed late to complete the job. Everyone sacrificed for the good of the whole and it ended up being an effective team-building exercise. They also agreed that they did not want to be in a similar situation in the future, so they retooled the process to avoid last minute fire drills (p. 73).

Tangible Gifts: As the name suggests, some individuals are motivated by gifts. The gifts do not have to be expensive; the key is the thoughtfulness behind the gift. For example, if you have an employee for whom gifts are important, you should take the time to learn the types of activities they enjoy, such as sporting events. Chapman and White discuss the two key components of effective tangible rewards: First, make sure the employee appreciates gifts, and second make sure the gift is of value to them personally. For example, if the person is a baseball fan, tickets to his or her favorite team's game would be a home run (pun intended).

Physical Touch: Chapman and White say many people value physical touch. This is obviously a sensitive topic in the work place. But individuals who value physical touch are looking for a "high five" when they have done a good job, or perhaps a pat on the back. They are more likely to give hugs and appreciate hugs in return. Given today's focus on sexual harassment, the application of physical touch requires careful observance of each employee's comfort-level with various types of touch. If you are someone who naturally shows appreciation in physical ways, such as hugs or pats on the back, be sure your employees are comfortable with such actions. Discomfort can be observed when employees get tense or move away. To avoid problems, you can also ask them before proceeding with a physical gesture. For employees who appreciate touch, a "high five" can be more effective than verbal recognition or tangible gifts (p. 93-102).

All employees value each of these ways of showing appreciation to some extent, but typically each person has a primary language that is most important to them. Since we tend to show appreciation the way we prefer to receive it, we can totally miss the mark with a teammate, even though we value that person's efforts. Therefore, as a manager and leader, you must closely observe your employees to identify what is most important to them and then tailor your recognition appropriately. You can also start by asking them questions, or by observing how they show appreciation to others. If you see an individual who often buys small gifts for others, you can quickly assess that gifts are important to them.

> **All employees value each of these ways of showing appreciation to some extent, but typically each person has a primary language that is most important to them.**

Since transitions and change can be hard for people to adopt, it is important to give people recognition for their successes. Do that and your effort will be more successful.

Next we will take a look at the last letter in P.L.A.N., which is about the need to monitor an effort after it is deployed.

N = Need to Monitor and Control

Have you ever been a part of launching a new initiative and then never heard another word about it? Or has someone told you about the importance of a new product or process, but it was never measured or discussed again? If so, how likely were you to invest your time and energy in that effort? Not very, I suspect. I've been there myself.

The reality is that employees focus on what their managers are monitoring through measurements and rewards. No matter how great a new program might be, if there is no way to monitor and control it, it will not be successful. Therefore, within the "How" P.L.A.N., the "N" stands for the need to monitor and control an effort. There are many tools outlined below that can be leveraged to assist with this critical step.

Develop clear measurements: How will your effort be measured? If you can't measure progress, it will be impossible to monitor results.

Connection to employee incentives: Is your program connected to employee incentives? If not, employees and managers may not pay attention to it.

Monitoring techniques: Assuming you have measurements and ways to incentivize the right behaviors, then you can use the following ideas to control results.

The first idea is auditing. Typically, this is done by either an internal or external team. Depending on the size of an organization, this could be a permanent group, usually housed outside the business to ensure impartiality. Auditors will often observe an effort based on standard operating procedures or outlined processes to ensure adherence. In some businesses, the process of auditing is critical to legal compliance, such as in banking. There are many laws regulating the interactions of branch employees, and auditors are employed to ensure adherence to the laws.

> No matter how great a new program might be, if there is no way to monitor and control it, it will not be successful.

The second idea is testing. Once an initiative has been deployed, testing employees on their knowledge of process and procedures can help you know to what degree employees are truly adopting the plan. Testing can be done by other employees or electronically. Most compliance training today is followed by pass/fail tests to ensure comprehension, and employees have to review training until the test is passed.

Whichever method you choose to monitor and control your changes, the key is to be consistent.

The third idea is a survey. This method can also be used to gauge how much people understand about an initiative, and to assess actual adoption levels. Surveys are also great tools to identify where additional improvements can be made in a process or procedure.

Whichever method you choose to monitor and control your changes, the key is to be consistent. Too often this important step is missed as companies move on to the next effort. The result is reduced progress or stalled plans.

Overall, leveraging the P.L.A.N. system will ensure that you have defined the right "How," gained necessary leadership support, ensured employee adoption, and have the right tools in place to maintain and improve your efforts in the long-term.

Next we will take a closer look how to leverage some of the Lean and Six Sigma tools when defining your "How."

There is surely nothing

quite so useless as

doing with great efficiency

what should not be done at all.

— Peter Drucker,
Managing for Business Effectiveness

CHAPTER 4

Define the "How" with Lean and Six Sigma Tools

Six Sigma and Lean offer very useful tools and approaches to remove unnecessary elements of business practices to improve productivity. I've met many people who think they are too complicated to leverage, or that hours of training are required to use these techniques. Well, if you are one of those people, I'm here to offer you a different perspective.

There certainly are components of Six Sigma and Lean that require in-depth training, a statistician, or even an expert in the methodologies. But, sadly, I've seen many people shy away from using the tools altogether because of a perception they all require training or certification to use. The reality is that many of the concepts we'll review in this chapter are relatively simple and straightforward to leverage in a change initiative.

Therefore, this chapter will provide a high-level overview of key Six Sigma tools and several Lean concepts to show how you can use them to develop and execute your P.L.A.N. We will review each step in the Six Sigma DMAIC approach and real world examples to help you better understand how these tools can be used to effectively develop the "How."

We will begin by defining the Six Sigma "DMAIC" process. DMAIC stands for Define, Measure, Analyze, Improve, and Control. The power of the DMAIC approach is that it requires you to think critically about a problem before jumping to the solution. All too often, managers or employees want to jump to the solution without digging deep to understand the core problem.

The challenge with jumping too fast to a solution is that you could be fixing the wrong problem, as depicted in the following example.

If you are caught speeding, you might immediately tell yourself that the solution is to not speed as much. But if you take a few moments to think about why you were speeding, you might find that there is a deeper reason.

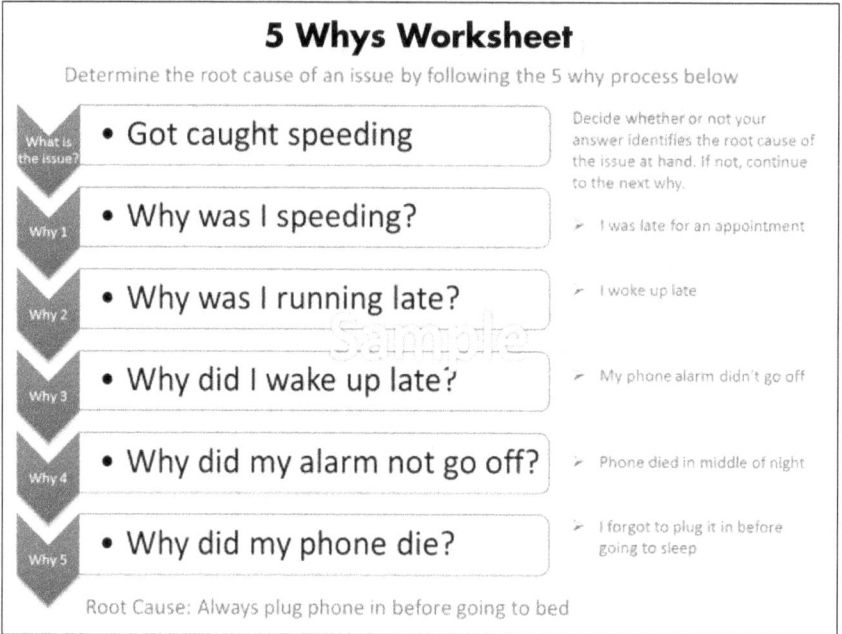

The Define Stage

The initial step in the Six Sigma DMAIC approach is to define the problem. The sample project charter outlined in Chapter 2 is typically the first component of the Define stage. The project charter usually evolves throughout the course of an initiative and includes elements such as the problem statement, goal, scope, customer input, and more. The Define stage outlines the "What" within the business case, including the rationale, problem statements, and the high-level "How." The "How" includes people, process, risks, key metrics, scope, and timeline.

As mentioned in the previous chapter, a cross-functional team should be engaged to help in this early stage as subject matter experts. Typically, if the team is helping to define the problem, they will be more engaged in the development and execution of the solution.

Another key benefit of leveraging Six Sigma is that it helps ensure that all facets of an initiative have been considered. I've seen efforts fail due to risk-related blind spots or lack of appropriate stakeholder approval. An initiative might move to the "Improve" stage, but if all stakeholders have not been considered, the team might have to go back to the Define stage. The Six Sigma DMAIC approach along with Lean provide ways to avoid that problem.

Within the Define phase, the key tools to help improve the "What" are as follows:

Project Charter: This tool is described in Chapter 2. It documents the business case, the problem statement, the project scope, the voice of the customer, the project goal/objective, the primary/secondary metrics, the cost of not improving, and the timeline.

Voice of Customer (VOC): This is essential to the effort. In strategic planning efforts, the customer could be internal as well as external. It's important to understand who your customers are, including their needs, and what—if any—data is available. VOC will help you understand what is critical to customers. In Six Sigma, this is often referred to as CTQ, or Critical to Quality. It is essentially the customer requirements of a product or service. An example of VOC might be, "I need better customer service," and the key barrier to that goal might be a computerized answering system that takes too long to get clients to the right support person. The CTQ would be to get customers to the right support person within one minute.

Pareto Distribution: The graph, Reasons for Customer Dissatisfaction: Pareto, on the following page shows the observed characteristics based on frequency, from largest to smallest, as in the diagram Current State: The Sub Shop on the following page.

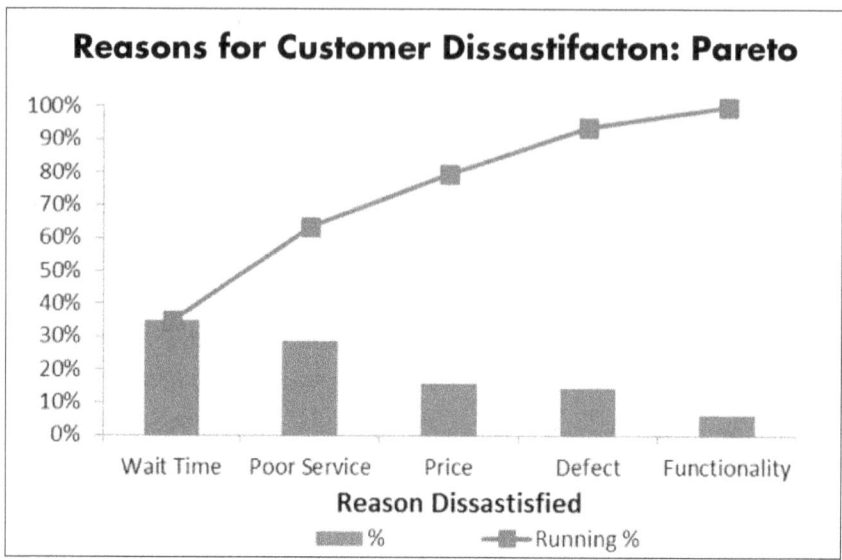

High-Level Process Map: Should the initiative involve improving a process (which most do), outlining the current process at a high level is very helpful for identifying existing gaps, as the example below shows (using a fictitious sub sandwich shop's process):

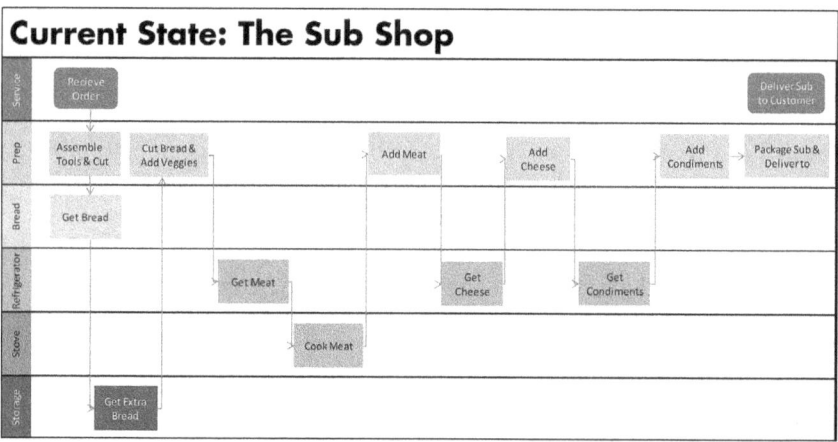

In this simple process outlined above, we can quickly identify what appear to be extra steps in the process of receiving and making an order. The design of this chart is typically referred to as "Swim Lanes" since it resembles swimming pool laps. An even simpler example is found below, using a fictitious intra-business referral process:

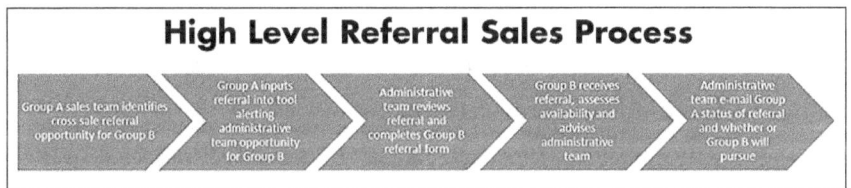

In the simple real-world process shown above, if a customer complains to the contact person in Group A that they are frustrated for not hearing from anyone in Group B, we know there is a breakdown in this process.

Small breakdowns in the process can end up adding a lot of redundancy in effort. The administration team could be a hindrance to processing referrals because of poor workflow management in that area. That could cause delays in communications with Group B. Or, the problem could be a technology breakdown, in which the tools are not working efficiently. The problem could be a misaligned incentive plan that doesn't reward Group B for Group A's referrals, thereby causing Group B to not respond in a timely manner, if at all. Possibly the challenges are due to lack of leadership focus or insufficient rewards for the effort required. The list of root causes could be extensive depending on the organization. Regardless of the cause, a simple map, such as the one above, can help pinpoint the core problem.

The Measure Stage

Once you have defined the improvement opportunity, the next step in the DMAIC approach is Measure. The Measure step is what differentiates Six Sigma from many other approaches. Six Sigma focuses on collecting and analyzing data, with a premise that it is very difficult to improve a process or product if you can't measure it. This concept is not new, but it's surprising how many leaders manage by "gut instinct" in today's data-rich age.

To be successful at achieving your stated goals, you need to be able to measure and identify success.

While I taught Six Sigma, the question I received most often was, "Why don't more companies or enterprises apply a continuous improvement approach like Six Sigma given that best-in-class companies have proven they work?" The answer is most often *limited time* and, secondly, *lack of expertise.* Time is the nemesis of most leaders and managers in today's fast-paced, ultra-competitive world. Although a continuous improvement approach can save time in the long run, limited capacity prevents leaders from reaching for long-term benefits.

We will assume that your company supports the effort to leverage data to improve your company efforts. Therefore, to be successful at achieving your stated goals, you need to be able to measure and identify success. This gives you the ability to recognize and reward improvements, and also to identify failures. Since it can be difficult to determine what will be measured in strategic efforts, we'll review the possible areas.

If you have identified the primary and secondary metrics in the project charter, those are good places to start. A few common tools are listed below, but if you would like more detailed information, many websites and books are readily available on the topic. Essentially, you want to establish a baseline for your initiative. You also need quantitative or qualitative evidence that proves progress (or not) toward your goals. These results can be leveraged in the next Six Sigma phase of analysis.

Using a Pareto chart in the Measure stage is an excellent approach. This is based on the Pareto, or 80/20 Principle. It is a very useful tool named after Italian economist Vilfredo Pareto. Pareto noted that 20 percent of the population was receiving 80 percent of the income. Joseph Juran expanded the idea to other instances where the 80/20 rule could be applied, and he named the principle after Pareto.

Based on my twenty years of business experience, I've found that it's uncanny how often the 80/20 principle is visible, especially within strategic decision discussions where 80 percent is often the target (due to the need to make estimations, 100 percent is not achievable). Essentially, a Pareto chart provides a visual depiction of information in a manner that helps us assess if the 80/20 principle will pinpoint where to focus your efforts. Based on my experience in companies of all sizes—from large corporations to small businesses—resources are always limited. Therefore, leveraging a

Pareto chart to determine which 20 percent to focus on so that you can fix 80 percent of your problem is incredibly useful.

Creating a Pareto Chart

When creating a Pareto chart, your data should be arranged from most common to least common. Microsoft Excel can be used to create a Pareto chart if you set the data up correctly. For example, let's say you surveyed your lost customers to determine the reason they no longer buy from you. The table below depicts a summary of the information gathered.

Lost Customer Reason	Count	Percentage	Running percentage
Price	120	40%	40%
Poor Service	110	37%	77%
Online Capability	30	10	87%
Geographic Move	20	7%	93%
Functionality	20	7%	100%
Total Count	**300**		

Then you can use the Excel bar-chart function to highlight the lost-customer reason columns to create your initial chart. Then, change the running percent to a line to produce a chart like the one below.

In addition to the number of instances in each category, the cumulative percentage of the total is shown as a number and as a line graph. This provides the quickest way to see if the principle applies.

In the example above, the first category makes up 40 percent of the lost business. If you add poor service, the total goes up to 77 percent. Therefore, you can conclude that approximately 80 percent of your customers are leaving because of price competitiveness or poor service. Thus, if you fix those two problems, you should see significant improvement in customer retention.

Scatter Diagrams

Scatter diagrams are a fancy name for providing a graphical presentation of data to determine if any statistical relationships exist. Scatter plots are useful when you have continuous data. Continuous data exists on a continuum, such as height, weight, length, time, etc. Continuous data is different from discrete data, which has finite values, such as a number of questions in a survey. Although scatter plots can depict a relationship between variables, they do not indicate cause and effect. Therefore, scatter diagrams are useful to visually identify if some other type of relationship exists or not. You can see this in the following graphic comparing hours playing video games in relation to grade-point averages.

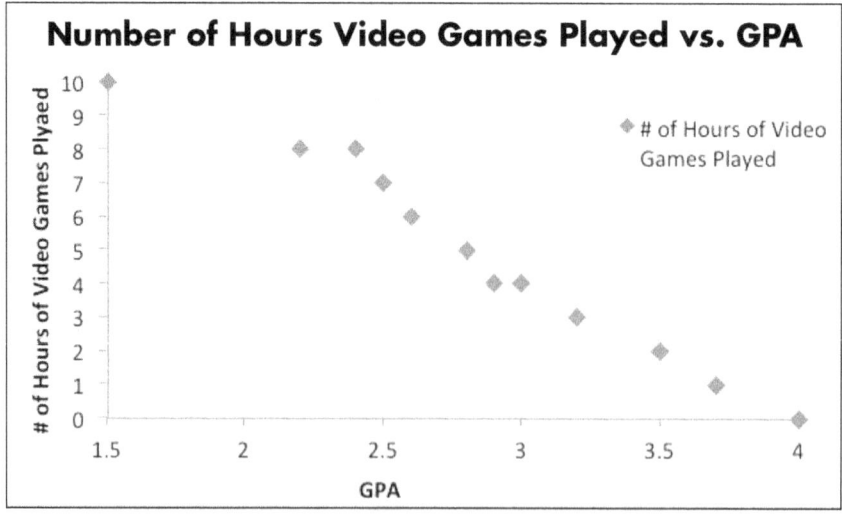

In this example, the arrow helps depict a negative correlation since the GPA (x value) is decreasing as the number of hours of playing video games (y value) is increasing. This does not prove that lower GPAs are *caused* by more hours playing video games; further analysis is needed to understand the specific reasons why GPAs were lower. Video game hours *could* be a cause, but lower GPAs could also be caused by other factors, such as a family crisis, difficult subject matters, job demands, etc.

Benchmarking

This involves gathering best-in-class business data specific to your goal. For example, if you are looking to improve your customer satisfaction results, you could compare your results to other companies in your industry that demonstrate best-in-class customer satisfaction results.

I've known of executives in large companies who met with leaders in other companies to better understand how they achieved better customer satisfaction or employee retention results. Benchmarking can be done for all sorts of factors ranging from customer satisfaction, product quality, employee engagement, turnover, etc. There are companies that provide online customer satisfaction indexes by industry, such as the American Customer Satisfaction Index (ACSI). Each year, various rankings of companies in certain categories are published. This information can be used to set a target within your company. For example, Southwest Airlines is often rated highest for overall customer satisfaction. Whether you are in the airline business or not, you can study how they satisfy their customers and then implement similar efforts in your business.

Run Charts

Run charts are a bit more complicated to leverage, but essentially they are graphical depictions of data displayed over time. They can be used for data involving costs, time, volume, customer satisfaction, and more. Run charts are useful to detect patterns and stability. A simple example, shown on next page, plots the number of daily errors. In this example, there seems to be a pattern of increasing errors weekly. With this information, you'd want to understand the underlying reasons for the pattern. For example, are there certain employees working on the days when the errors are the highest? Or, is the volume of productivity significantly higher on certain days? Within the next DMAIC phase, "Analyze," you would determine the root cause for the errors and in the "Improve" phase you develop how to fix the process.

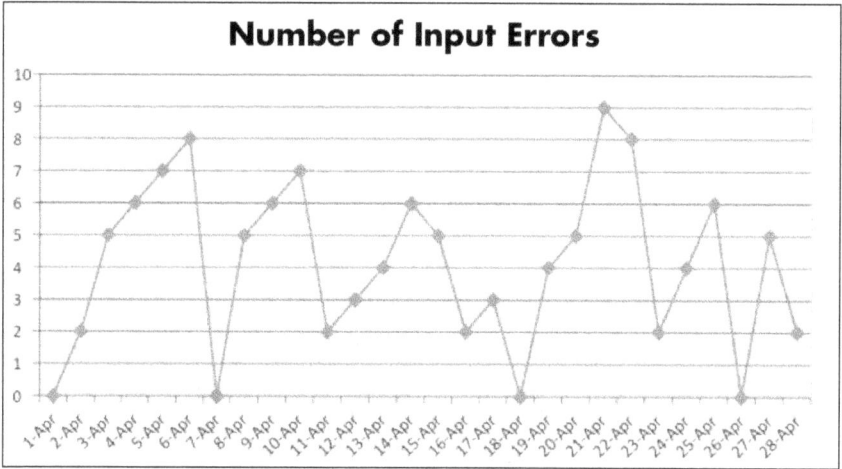

Measurement System Evaluation (MSA)

This is the method of understanding how much variation exists within the measurement tools you are using. For example, if you are going to use a one-foot ruler to measure height, there will likely be variation in the total height each time the person is measured. Using a better tool for this application, such as seven feet of flexible measuring tape will likely produce consistent measures.

Rolled Throughput Yield (RTY)

RTY is the probability that a single unit can pass through a series of process steps free of defects. Below is a simple example of how to leverage this concept to assess the capability of a three-step process. (Fewer defects means there is a more predictable process capable of producing your desired outcome.)

Step 1: 100 parts passed through a process and 80 "good" parts left the process (scrapped 20)

Step 2: These 80 parts passed through step 2 with 75 "good" parts passing (5 scrapped)

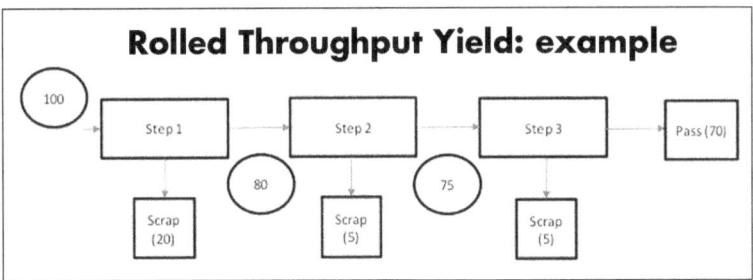

Step 3: 75 parts pass through with 70 parts passing (5 scrapped).

Since the manager only cares about "what goes out the door" the process they are most concerned with is the last one in Step 3. They feel they had a great day, since there were only five scrapped parts and they report a "yield" of 93 percent (70/75).

Is the yield really 93 percent? Not if you consider the entire process. The 93 percent yield did not consider the scrapped parts that steps 1 and 2 created. The upfront processes can sometimes be unknown to managers and only known by the folks on the line.

Here is how this manager should be measuring the performance of the process using RTY.

Step 1 had a daily yield of 80 percent (80/100) while Step 2 had a daily yield of 94 percent (75/80), and finally, Step 3 had a daily yield of 93 percent (70/75).

So, to calculate RTY we simply multiply these yields together giving us a composite yield for the day. Doing this gives us:

80 percent x 94 percent x 93 percent = 70 percent

The opportunity for improvement is great, considering a yield of 70 percent vs. 93 percent.

Cost of Poor Quality (COPQ)

COPQ, as its name implies, is all costs associated with defective outcomes. Below is a list of sample costs that are easy to detect, as well as costs associated with lost opportunities:

Easy-to-detect costs associated with bad quality:

- Rejects or returns

- Inspection

- Repairs or rework

- Warranty

Lost opportunity costs (harder to quantify, but very real in most scenarios):

- Lost sales

- Late delivery

- Long set-up or cycle times

- Expediting costs

- Lost customers

- Employee safety

- Excessive inventory

The costs associated with poor quality can be a significant factor in building a case for improvements, since all companies are typically in favor of reducing costs. Quality issues with products and services have a cost, and this measure can help you quantify it.

The Analyze Stage

Once you have identified and quantified your business goal, the next critical step is to pause and analyze what the information is telling you. Remember that implementing Six Sigma is an analytical effort; hence, the third step in the DMAIC approach is titled "Analyze."

The essence of this phase is to leverage tools that help you better understand the situation, determine root causes, and validate theories. You will want to use available data to reinforce the validity of the effort. While individuals will always have opinions, data can help quantify and validate hypotheses. If you change a process or program, the proposed result will show up in the data. Some of the common tools leveraged in the Analyze phase include:

Root Cause Analysis:
Five Whys, and Cause and Effect Diagrams

Determining the root cause of an issue is essential, since fixing the wrong problem will be a waste of your limited resources. The initial situation could even be worse due to lost time. I like both tools because they are simple and straightforward to use.

To utilize the Five Whys tool, once you identify your problem, you simply ask "Why" five times to get at the core problem. An example of this may include the following:

- **What is the issue?** Customers are getting poor service.

- Why 1: Why are customers getting poor service? The wait to get service is long.

> Determining the root cause of an issue is essential, since fixing the wrong problem will be a waste of your limited resources.

- Why 2: Why are the wait times long? The long wait lines are due to staff taking longer to process requests.

- Why 3: Why is the staff taking longer to process requests? The computers were updated and training has not been fully completed.

- Why 4: Why has training not been fully completed? The store does not have enough staff to allow for training.

- Why 5: Why does the store not have enough staff to allow for training to be completed? They need extra help to assist with employees going off stage to complete the training.

- **Root Cause:** Additional staffing is required to allow for employees to be fully trained on new systems so they can service customers faster.

The second tool is a "cause and effect" diagram, also known as a "fishbone" diagram for its resemblance to a fishbone. This approach applies a framework to help dig into the cause of the undesired outcome. The tool first identifies broad categories that could be causing a problem, such as a poor-quality product. Then within each category, you outline all possible primary and sub-causes. A blank diagram can be very effective in a brainstorming session with stakeholders or users. You may want to pre-fill the categories to spark discussion and then ensure all possible causes are captured. The sample below includes potential causes for a poor-quality product. The ends of the "bones" on the fish can be whatever categories are applicable to the situation you are examining. I've listed some of the most common ones, but others could include the environment, regulations, or measurement.

> **This approach applies a framework to help dig into the cause of the undesired outcome.**

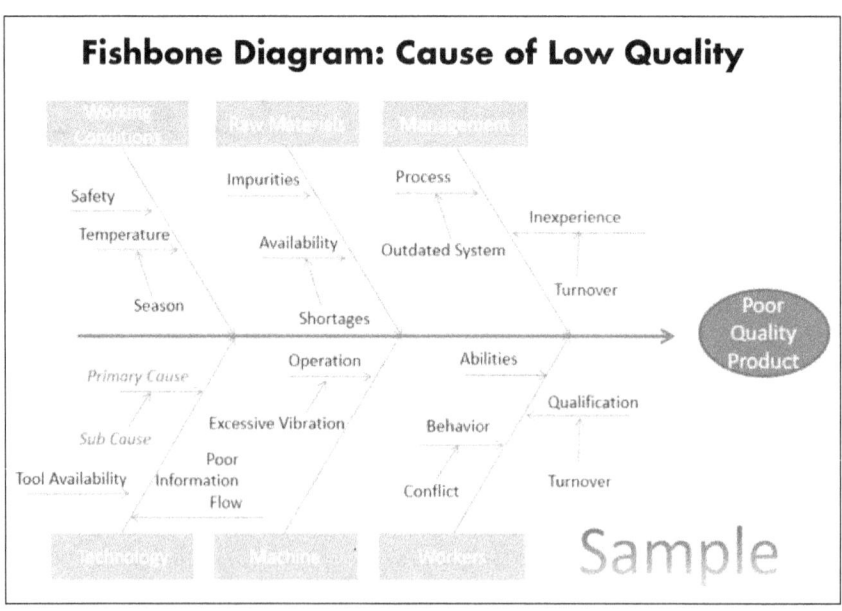

Fishbone Diagram: Cause of Low Quality

In the example above, a cause for a poor-quality product is fluctuating temperature that is dependent on the season. If that turns out to be the most significant cause, temperature controls could be needed to improve the product quality. An important point when leveraging this type of tool, or any tool within the Analyze phase, is to hold the team back from solving "problems" too quickly. As we saw with the "5 Why's," digging for the root cause is essential to avoid solving the wrong problem. Although this concept seems straight-forward and common sense, I can't count how many times I've been a part of organizations that are solving the wrong problem. This almost always occurred when underlying systems were broken and the teams were disengaged due to discouragement. Many times, people worked to solve the wrong problem because of a short-term focus, especially in public companies driving toward a quarterly Wall Street goal.

For example, I've witnessed average-performance businesses reduce staff to inefficient levels in order to make quarterly numbers look better. The root cause for poor performance was not too much staff. In twenty years, I was never a part of an organization that had excess capacity to take on more work. In fact, no matter the industry, size of business, or department, all of them always had more work than they could get done with existing staff working

Many times, people worked to solve the wrong problem because of a short-term focus, especially in public companies driving toward a quarterly Wall Street goal.

extra hours every week. Therefore, the poor performance was not due to too many staff. The "poor" performance was typically due to unrealistic revenue growth goals or broken systems that produced low-quality products or services.

Another tool to help you get to the root cause of a problem is a detailed end-to-end process map. Let's look at that more closely.

Detailed End-to-End Process Mapping

A high-level process map is typically included within the Define phase, like the examples included on earlier pages. In the Analyze phase, you will likely want to include a step-by-step walk through of the process, similar to the example below. In the example below, we see the different teams impacted by a sample referral sales process. The example provided is still high-level, but we can see inefficiencies in terms of multiple teams handling a referral, and many customer touch points. Depending on how much time it takes to complete each of these steps, the process could magnify the inefficiency and impact on the customer. For example, if the administration team took a week to enter the referral into the tool, or if the customer is expecting a quick response (which most are), this will cause customer and employee dissatisfaction. Outlining the steps in a process helps identify inefficiencies or waste in the process.

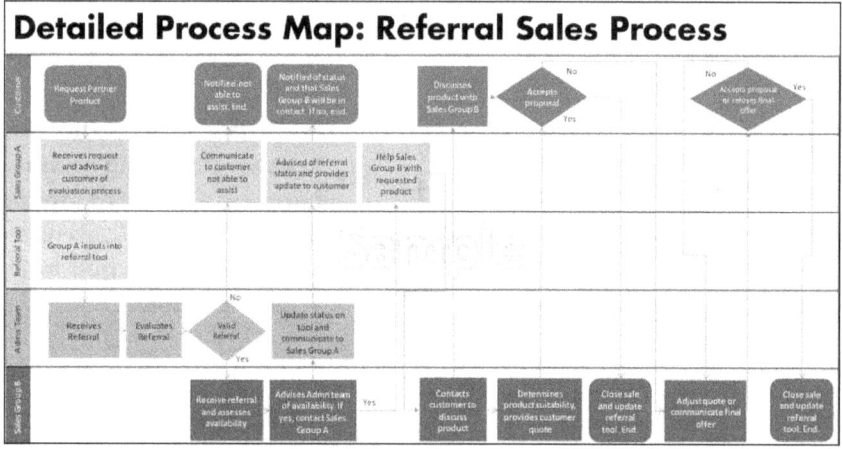

Failure Mode Effect Analysis (FMEA)

This tool has a fancy name, but it's straight-forward to use as a tool to identify and categorize potential failure points within a process, product, or service. The failure "mode" identifies ways that something might fail. As we see in the example on next page, failures are prioritized according to how serious the consequences are (effect), frequency of occurrence and ability to detect.

Typically, FMEAs are compiled by a cross-functional team of stakeholders. I've been part of these discussions, and engaging all parties who are part of a process is essential to ensure the quantitative assessment is as accurate as possible.

Failure Mode Effect Analysis: example

Process Step	Potential Failure Mode	Potential Failure Effect	SEV[1]	Potential Causes	OCC[2]	Current Process Controls	Det[3]	RPN[4]	Action Recommended
What is the Step?	In what ways can the step go wrong?	What is the impact on the customer if the failure mode is not prevented or corrected?	How severe is the effect on the customer?	What causes the step to go wrong or how could it fail?	How frequently is the cause likely to occur?	What are the existing controls that either prevent the failure mode from occurring or detect it should it occur?	How probable is detection of the failure mode or its cause?	Risk priority number calculated as SEV x OCC x DET	What are the actions for reducing the occurrence of the cause or for improving its detection? Provide actions on all high RPNs and on severity ratings of 9 or 10.
ATM Pin Authentication	Unauthorized access	*Unauthorized cash withdrawal *Very dissatisfied customer	9	Lost or stolen ATM card	3	Block ATM card after two failed attempts	3	81	Require pins be updated every 6 months to prevent theft
	Authentication failure	Annoyed customer	3	Network failure	5	Install additional network options should one fail	5	75	
Dispense Cash	Cash not disbursed	Dissatisfied customer	7	ATM out of cash	7	Internal alert ATM low on cash	4	196	Increase minimum cash threshold limit on ATMs to prevent out-of-cash instances
	Account debited but no cash disbursed	Very dissatisfied customer	8	*Transaction failure *Network issue	3	Install additional network options should one fail	4	96	
	Extra cash dispensed	Bank loses money	8	*Bills stuck to each other *Bills stacked incorrectly	2	Two person rule while loading cash in ATM	3	48	

1. **Severity:** Severity of impact of failure event. It is scored on a scale of 1 to 10. A high score is assigned to high-impact events while a low score is assigned to low-impact events.

2. **Occurrence:** Frequency of occurrence of failure event. It is scored on a scale of 1 to 10. A high score is assigned to frequently occurring events while events with low occurrence are assigned a low score.

3. **Detection:** Ability of process control to detect the occurrence of failure events. It is scored on a scale of 1 to 10. A failure event that can be easily detected by the process control is assigned a low score while a high score is assigned to an inconspicuous event.

4. **Risk priority number:** The overall risk score of an event. It is calculated by multiplying the scores for severity, occurrence and detection. An event with a high RPN demands immediate attention while events with lower RPNs are less risky.

The Improve Stage

The next step in the DMAIC approach is "Improve." This is the step in which you finally get to focus on fixing the process, program, or whatever it is that is broken. If you were successful in getting the team to be patient and disciplined in the previous steps, you will have a wealth of factual information to help develop a lasting solution! This result is the brilliance of improving processes with Lean and Six Sigma tools. Let's consider some common tools leveraged within the Improve phase.

Design of Experiments (DOE)

A designed experiment is a test (or series of tests) that enables the experimenter to compare two or more methods to determine which is better, or to determine levels of controllable factors that optimize a process or minimize the variability.

DOE can be very complicated, but the common example of making popcorn illustrates the general concept. The goal is to find the most efficient way to make popcorn on the stove. The outcome will be measured by the highest percentage of kernels popped (popped kernels / total kernels). Key factors include:

- How long to cook the popcorn
- What level of heat to use on the stove
- Which brand of popcorn to use

DOE can be very effective at improving procedures. For example, each run involves popping two hundred kernels of corn. After popping, you measure the number of popped kernels for the different factors to see which combination produces the best outcome. Your results may look something like this:

Run	Popcorn Brand	Cooking Time	Level of Heat	Popped
1	Orville Redenbacher	5 minutes	medium	75%
2	Orville Redenbacher	5 minutes	high	85%
3	Orville Redenbacher	6 minutes	medium	80%
4	Orville Redenbacher	6 minutes	high	88%
			OR Average	82%
5	Farm Fresh	5 minutes	medium	83%
6	Farm Fresh	5 minutes	high	86%
7	Farm Fresh	6 minutes	medium	84%
8	Farm Fresh	6 minutes	high	89%
			FF Average	85.5%

A quick analysis of the above runs would tell us that the Farm Fresh popcorn cooked on high heat seemed to produce the highest yield at 89 percent. For a stronger confidence level, you would want to repeat the runs to ensure consistent results.

Mistake Proofing (Poka Yoke)

Poka yoke is a Japanese term that simply means "mistake proofing." A *poka yoke* device is a system or tool that is used to help prevent errors. Often referred to as "error-proofing," *poka yoke* is the first step in error-proofing a system, and it can be applied to all environments. A simple example of a *poka yoke* is a computer warning such as the one pictured right, which suggests that files may be harmful to your computer. It could save you from downloading a virus onto your PC.

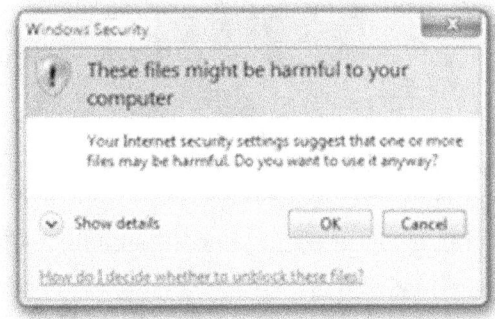

Deming Cycle: Plan, Do, Check, and Act

All good books on statistics and Six Sigma typically include a mention of William Edwards Deming, who was instrumental in leveraging statistics within quality control efforts. One of his best-known tools was called the "Deming Cycle of Plan: Do, Check, and Act." Deming's cycle is described below in regards to what it is and how to implement it.

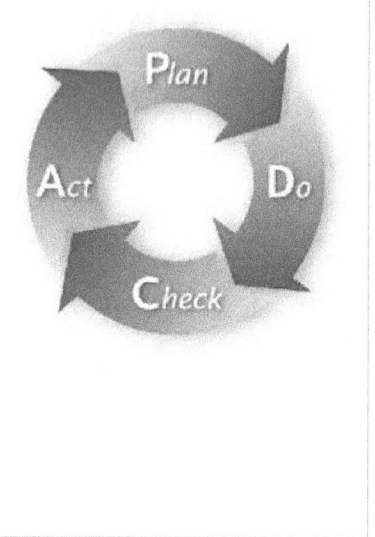

What: The model is an approach for repeating a continuous improvement methodology that can be repeated again and again.

Plan: Identify an improvement opportunity and plan a change.

Do: Test what you plan to change on a small scale.

Check: Examine results of test and identify areas of improvement.

Act: Take action based on test results and learning. If the test did not produce the desired results, go back through the cycle again with a new plan. If efforts were successful, go back through the cycle to identify additional improvements. Repeat the entire process indefinitely.

Deming's approach can be used when starting a new project or looking to improve an existing process or product. The power of his model is that it is simple to use when implementing any change effort.

End-State Process Mapping

End-state process mapping incorporates improvements made to streamline an effort or reduce waste. Taking a second look at the sample referral sales process from the earlier example, we can see inefficiencies resulting from multiple teams handling one referral at many customer touch points. Analyzing the situation may reveal that the administration team was creating a bottle neck between the sales teams, adding up to ten days to the process and additional customer contacts. Therefore, a significant improvement to reduce errors and wasted time could be to reconfigure the process or tools so as to eliminate the need for an intermediary (administration team) between the sales teams, as depicted in the graphic below. This proposal may involve eliminating jobs, which in my experience is always difficult, especially for the impacted team. Many times, employees can be repositioned in other areas so the impact on people is minimal. Regardless, the end-state process map should reflect the project goals. In this case, if the goal was to improve the referral process by reducing the total cycle time, the proposal below should meet the goal.

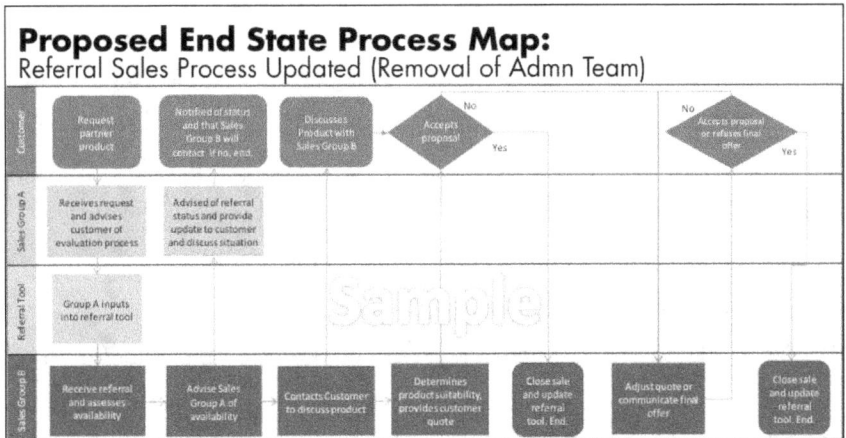

Proposed End State Process Map:
Referral Sales Process Updated (Removal of Admn Team)

Overall, the goal of the Improve phase is to implement changes that achieve the initial project charter goals of improving customer satisfaction, reducing costs, and improving product quality, etc. Once changes have been implemented, the next and final DMAIC phase is "Control."

The Control Stage

The Six Sigma Control stage is simple, but not easy to implement. It is often executed poorly, if at all. However, it is critical for ensuring that all previous efforts were not wasted, and that the changes made will be consistently executed in the future. Using control tools is essential for company cultures that are focused on continuous improvement. It helps them to consistently execute the "How."

Chapter 6 covers tools that help monitor and control efforts, so here I will focus on a couple of Lean tools that can also be leveraged in your "How" P.L.A.N.

Lean tools can be leveraged to quantify areas for improvement, such as the "Five S's" and Value-Stream Mapping outlined below.

The Five S's

This is a simple, but effective tool that stands for Sort, Straighten, Shine, Standardize, and Sustain. Organizing a workspace provides a foundation to make necessary improvements and identify waste within a process. Waste can be quantified by excess materials, waiting or transport time, errors due to inefficiencies, or poor quality, etc. Within the Five S's, it's important to ensure that everything has a place and that everything is in its place. It also requires cleanliness and standards that are sustainable.

Lean Value-Stream Mapping

This is an effective tool to help a team see workflow and information for a specific set of processes. Most Lean practitioners utilize value-stream maps as a tool to identify waste and to reduce process cycle times (the length of time it takes to complete a task). Identifying these items helps to identify areas for process improvement.

A potential value-stream map of a patient's movement within a hospital emergency room is shown below. The waiting time, which would be considered a waste, is highlighted in between each step. Below the map we see the measured processing and wait times. Since wasted time often creates customer dissatisfaction and is expensive, a simple value-stream map like the one below can help identify the areas where the largest improvements can be made.

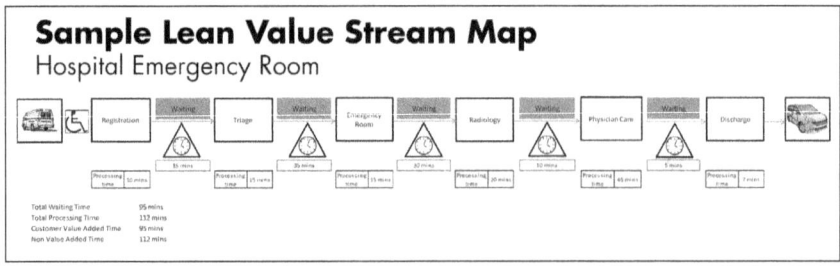

Although I realize this chapter contains a lot of technical content, I'm hopeful you will find it a useful resource and consider applying the Six Sigma and Lean tools in your efforts. There are many more detailed resources online, and extensive training is available should you want to become an expert.

Next, we will take a look at the importance of effective communications when deploying change initiatives.

Strategy is formulated at all levels

of the organization, and to be successful,

it needs to be clearly communicated

at all levels as well.

— Lafley & Martin, *Playing to Win*

CHAPTER 5

The Importance of Effective Communications

Have you ever been confused by your company's messaging on a certain topic? Have you wondered what it may mean for you in your job? Have you felt unsure if the change was good or bad? Or has a manager ever told you to ignore the messaging because it wasn't important. If so, you've experienced ineffective communications.

The truth is that effective communication is critical to the execution of a strategy or initiative. Many business authors have suggested that strategies need to be clearly communicated for an organization to be effective. Clear communication is the result of explaining a strategy simply, and in a meaningful way. And good communication helps business teams understand how they will be impacted by changes. Yet based on my experience, many messaging efforts fall short of these expectations, for several reasons.

I love the phrase "less is more." It certainly applies to communication. When crafting a message, it's important to limit it to the essential components, keeping it simple for your audience. Albert Einstein reinforces this concept in his famous quote: "If you can't explain something simply, you don't understand it well." The better you understand a concept, the easier it is to summarize for others.

Simple Principles of Effective Messaging

When it comes to communicating change or strategies, repetition is important. It's how we learn as children, and as adults. I'm a big fan of Jeff Weiner, CEO at LinkedIn. He wrote one of the best articles I've seen on effective leadership communication. It's titled, "Just Because You Said it, Doesn't Make It So" (2014). In this article, Jeff reinforces the importance of keeping communication (and strategies) simple and repetitive. Jeff shared a story from a previous job where his boss, a senior executive, had delivered an edict to the team that rolled out new priorities for the company. After many months, the executive was discouraged that the team had not yet implemented his directives. He came to Jeff asking why. Jeff responded with the following commentary:

Clear communication is the result of explaining a strategy simply, and in a meaningful way.

> We rolled out four new dimensions on top of seven previously communicated priorities, thus creating essentially twenty-eight different initiatives. While the determination of the seven priorities was a highly collaborative effort, and subsequently well-received, none of the new dimensions and the implications of adding those to the priorities were previously socialized or vetted with the people responsible for executing them. There was no stack ranking of the pillars and their intersection with the priorities. There were no measurable objectives communicated that would enable us to track results. The overlay of the pillars created an entirely new set of inter-dependencies between teams, without any guidance on how to navigate those new relationships or time to create the right connective tissue. No additional process was put in place enabling us to report out on progress, identify blockers, and work together to resolve critical issues. [Long pause, big smile.] What could possibly go wrong? . . .
>
> . . . In retrospect, I could summarize the entire discussion by saying, 'As a senior executive, just because you said it, doesn't make it so.'
>
> I have come back to this anecdote countless times since, not only sharing the experience with leaders on my team so that they can avoid similar outcomes, but to remind myself of the same thing. It's a hard lesson to learn. After all, as senior executives, most of us are wired to believe that

if we say it, the team will just naturally execute it as we had envisioned. If management were only that simple.

We all need to be wary of avoiding the Ron Burgundy syndrome: On the surface, looking and sounding the part, but without providing the right discipline, focus, and ongoing context, appearing as nothing more than a talking head.

Jeff shared the following key pieces of advice that I agree with whole-heartedly:

Repetition: In order to effectively communicate you need to say it so many times you grow sick of hearing yourself say it.

Simplify the narrative: We are the stories that we tell. When communicating important new messages, try thinking of it as introducing a new narrative. The simpler, more relevant, and more inspirational the message, the more likely it is to resonate with its intended audience.

Also, be aware of how many objectives, priorities, and themes you've been communicating over time. With greater success comes greater scope and complexity, and this can lead to a larger number of important narratives that need to be shared with the team. However, people can only understand so many things at once. Try consolidating. Even more importantly, periodically and systematically try taking things off the list (easier said than done).

> **The simpler, more relevant, and more inspirational the message, the more likely it is to resonate with its intended audience.**

The fewer things you need to communicate, the more people will internalize the message and align themselves accordingly. And that will help you achieve success.

Explain the "why": Regardless of how senior you are, or how much authority you wield, just saying it won't magically make it happen. Your audience is busy (if not overwhelmed) by their own work. In order to get them to take notice, and far more importantly, to change behavior, it's essential that you provide the context for your message. They need to know why this initiative is so important, why is it a higher priority than what the team is currently working on, and why is it a better strategy than the one already in place.

Listen to your team: After explaining the "Why," it's critical that the team feels heard on the subject, especially when there is disagreement. Seek to understand everyone on the team. Because they are close to the work, they'll usually have a unique perspective that helps shape your own. The solutions and ideas will be more effective because you developed them together.

In addition to clarity, effective communication requires leadership endorsement, management support, and employee engagement. We will look at each of these elements next.

Building Leadership Endorsement

Leadership endorsement, when it comes to communication, means that your leaders have helped to develop and support key messaging. As a change manager for many years, I would always seek to include executives within the development and review of our communications. This added time to the process of development, although technology (such as voting tools in Outlook) can help to get approvals from executives faster. Holding live webinars can also help by bringing leaders together to finalize content in real-time.

Once the content has been developed and approved, getting leaders to deliver at least a portion of the message will help validate their support within the impacted team. Employees, especially in large organizations, are more likely to listen and adapt to a new initiative if they hear it from their manager. Although there can be many challenges engaging leaders and so-lidifying their support in terms of content and delivery, without it, your effort will be disadvantaged from the onset. If you struggle to get leaders to deliver a message in person, you can use signed written communications, such as email, printed letters, or simply including quotes from them in your own communication. Written forms are typically easier to manage than "live" forums. The best communication plans include both live and written components. And today, recording live is easy and effective for those not able to attend an actual forum.

You will need leadership support for your communications or you will have a difficult time engaging the team. In many organizations, leaders are managers. The management team can be a separate and important group to engage. Without leader support, your effort to execute a strategy will be disadvantaged.

Obtaining the Support of Managers

Once you have engaged your executive leadership in communications, your next step will be to ensure you have the support of all managers. If you have high-level leadership support, but your managers are not engaged, you will still have a difficult time reaching frontline employees. It's also not enough for managers to just "touch pass" a communication, such as forwarding an email with no comments; you will want them to understand the content, to truly support the effort, and to assist with adoption.

You will need leadership support for your communications or you will have a difficult time engaging the team.

This may require training managers first. I've developed separate communications for managers that they can deliver to their teams. At a minimum, you will want them to be well-versed in the subject, since they will typically be the first line of defense when employees have questions. I've experienced situations in which managers were not well informed of changes. In those cases, you can bet that their employees were not aware either.

Developing Employee Engagement

To build employee engagement with a new initiative or change, communication is critical. This requires you to effectively deliver the messages about the strategy, and to develop helpful training materials. Let's look at each of these more carefully.

Delivering Your Messages

Have you ever been a part of a large meeting during which a leader was announcing a new initiative and the delivery was so poor that you had a hard time paying attention? Sadly, this happens a lot, and it can hinder the launch of new efforts.

In many instances, as a leader of change, you may be asked to deliver communications directly to impacted employees. Once you have your message crafted—based on input from leaders, managers, and key employees—you should also invest time in your delivery.

Once you have your message crafted—based on input from leaders, managers, and key employees—you should also invest time in your delivery.

I was deathly afraid of presenting in public when I was young. As a freshman in college, my first presentation was so bad that my classmates could hardly look at me. Therefore, since public speaking was hard for me, I invested time in extra training and took advantage of opportunities to expand my comfort zone. If this is an area you'd like to grow in, I'd suggest you focus on the following components.

Preparation, preparation, preparation: I've given speeches to small and large groups. Delivering the information in an interesting and confident manner makes a huge difference in engaging your audience. But to do this, you have to prepare. In my opinion, many managers and leaders do not spend enough time developing or improving their presentation skills.

Eliminate filler words: The best presenters have mastered the art of using minimal or no filler words, such as um, ah, right, like, and so. In our culture, silence is uncomfortable, so we tend to fill silence with words. But you can train your mind to not say these words. I know this from experience. Practice not using them *outside of work,* since personal habits tend to sneak into professional settings.

Tell stories: When possible, telling stories will reinforce your message. Research has shown that people tend to retain stories better than abstract content, and stories make ideas more interesting.

Practice, practice, practice: When I need to deliver an important presentation to key stakeholders, I practice three or four times. Effective communication is more about nonverbal elements, such as your tone, body language, eye contact, and confidence (the "How"). Therefore, if you have mastered the content of your presentation (the "What"), you will be able to focus on the nonverbal components for a brilliant delivery!

Verify your effectiveness: After you deliver your presentation, you should verify that your audience received your intended message. A great technique to gauge your effectiveness is to have your receivers "mirror" back to you what you just said. Some refer to this as reflective listening. For example, I announce that we are going to have a new incentive program with three elements and then I describe each component. When I'm finished, I ask the audience to name the three elements I just described. If they can only recite two, then I might not have done a good job outlining all three. Communication is not an exact science, so asking your audience to repeat what you said can be extremely helpful. In my experience, it is safe to say that I needed to clarify some element of nearly every presentation. As you seek feedback, don't use the question, "Do you understand?" This will inevitably get heads bobbing, but it will not provide you with useful information about the effectiveness of your communication. Rather, have them paraphrase what you said so you can ensure comprehension.

Developing Effective Training Materials

Lastly, we will look at some tricks for developing effective training materials, and some pitfalls in that process.

Training materials are often the key to helping employees adopt a new model or initiative, but they can be tricky to develop. We need to include the details that future teams can reference while also being succinct enough to be effective. Throughout my career, I've had the opportunity several times to develop training materials in support of strategic initiatives. Let me share some of the common pitfalls I've seen.

Information overload: This happens when the process or product developer includes so much detail that the most important elements get lost in the messaging. I've seen this all too often in the new, lengthy "Quick Reference Guide" that is more than ten pages long and very complex. A lengthy guide often becomes a tool for management to reference when a specific situation comes up, rather than a useful tool for line employees. A quick reference guide should be just that: quick. Ideally, one page with only the critical elements of an initiative need to be noted. If a project, such as an incentive plan, requires ten pages to explain, it's likely too complicated.

Delivering too far in advance: Training that is delivered too far in advance of a change will be a waste of effort. Studies have shown that individuals do not retain new information they do not use. In fact, most training will not be retained if it is not applied within thirty days.

Avoiding Pitfalls

To help avoid some of these pitfalls, here are some tips from my bag of tricks.

Apply the "rule of three": In most cases, less is more, and applying the rule of three will help to ensure your training is effective. For example, apply this rule when communicating a new incentive plan. You would categorize all components within three categories: improve customer satisfaction, simplify efforts for employees, and increase revenue.

> Training that is delivered too far in advance of a change will be a waste of effort.

Schedule training at the right time: The optimal time to train employees is within thirty days of the initiative's roll-out. Since most training is not retained unless it's used right away, you should try to schedule training efforts close to the actual roll-out to be most effective.

Keep it simple: This concept is simple, not easy. Remember, less is more. Use pictures that convey ideas. Have others review the materials to remove unnecessary words. Evaluate what is the most critical information needed to properly train employees and cut everything else. Remember, less is more.

Obtain an end-user review: Prior to usage, have an end-user review your training materials. Have them look at factors such as ease-of-use and understandability. Taking this extra step prior to roll-out, and making necessary adjustments before training starts, can spare a lot of headaches down the road.

Overall, developing and delivering effective communications takes effort. You need to invest the time to ensure that communications are clear, concise, and simple to understand. Without such components, the best-planned initiative can fail.

In the next chapter, we will take another look at what it takes to execute strategies, including real-world examples of brilliance and failure.

Carefully crafted strategic initiatives

and plans are of little value

until they are executed successfully.

— Stettinius, Wood, Jr., Doyle & Colley. Jr.,
How to Plan and Execute Strategy

CHAPTER 6

Execute, Execute, Execute

"The end of a matter is better than its beginning,
and patience is better than pride."
— Ecclesiastes 7:8 NIV

Once you have determined the "How," are you done? Let's say you have a wonderful retirement plan. Is it worth anything if you don't do what you've planned? Of course not. The same goes in business. The best planning and communication in the world are useless unless the effort is executed successfully.

Despite repeated attempts to improve in this area of project execution, many companies continue to fall short. The question is why? In this chapter, we will look at what it takes to execute well by analyzing examples of brilliant and failed execution. We will see that developing and deploying the "How" requires more than the right strategy and policies; it also requires solid leadership, understanding customer expectations, and a supportive corporate culture.

What is "solid" leadership? As we'll see in the following example, it's leadership that is consistent with a strategy. It's also effective leadership, to the extent that the leaders are able to engage employees and get them to follow. If leaders are delivering an inconsistent message, either literally or by their actions, a strategy will likely fail.

Our first example demonstrates the difference strong leadership makes in executing strategies. In New England, where I live, there is a grocery store chain named Market Basket. They have a rather typical strategy of seeking to offer lower prices and better value; hence their slogan, "More for Your Dollar." They also treat everyone from employees, to customers, to suppliers as equals. One role is not more important than another.

Prior to the summer of 2014, I had only frequented the store on rare occasions. I felt like the products were priced well, but the stores were very crowded when I shopped there, and so I purchased most of my groceries elsewhere. Then an amazing thing happened during the summer of 2014.

Prior to that summer, Market Basket was reaching the brink of collapse due to long standing feuds between the owning families. But then an incredible business story started to unfold. One man's amazing leadership and seemingly flawless execution was displayed through the extreme loyalty of customers, suppliers, and employees. The business did so well, that a book was published about what occurred.

The best planning and communication in the world are useless unless the effort is executed successfully.

The book, *We are Market Basket*, describes the situation as follows "the story of a battle over the future of a company—a battle that pitted cousin against cousin, employees and customers against shareholders, and some say good against evil. The Market Basket story is the result of a combination of events that occurred over nearly a century. The history of the Market Basket would save New England; a loyalty to the Market Basket family that created fierce commitment among associates, customers, and vendors; a commitment to excellence that produced great discipline; and a belief in experience over textbook theory that resulted in a willingness to throw away the rulebook set forth by the board, scholars, or the media. Market Basket is unique. (Korschun & Welker, 2015)

In the summer of 2014, the company owners ousted the leader, a man named Arthur T. Demoulas. When they did that, the employees boycotted their employer. And when the employees boycotted, the customers and suppliers joined them in the boycott! For months during the boycott, the huge parking lots, typically overflowing with cars, were empty. The stores stopped carrying fresh produce, since it all had gone bad. Driving by these empty stores was eerie and miraculous at the same time. Everyone from top to bottom was unified, which made the boycott—and much needed change—effective.

The employees, suppliers, and customers of Market Basket—working together through an incredible boycott—ultimately fought and won for Arthur's reinstatement. When Arthur was reinstated later that summer, his return speech was probably the most heartfelt speech I've ever heard a business leader deliver to a company. He humbly thanked all his employees, suppliers, and the customers who had fought so hard for him to be reinstated. He was loyal to them and they were loyal to him.

Amazingly, the stores came back to full life almost instantaneously. That's when I became a loyal customer. I remember my first trip there, shortly after the reinstatement, and everyone was smiling because something amazing had just happened. As Arthur said, the success was shared and achieved by working together.

But it's important to remember that Arthur's extraordinary leadership prior to the crisis had ensured the loyalty of everyone. It was his long-term history of flawless execution that made him so popular. And, at the heart of his effective strategy execution was his ability to build high levels of employee engagement in the company.

Employee engagement is a buzzword, but it remains elusive to many companies today. Leaders talk a lot about it, and they say they understand the value it brings. They talk about employees taking ownership to solve problems, reduced employee turnover, higher customer satisfaction, etc. Yet the fact remains that very few companies achieve a fraction of the level of employee engagement that Market Basket achieved. In fact, Gallup reported that only 33 percent of *all* US employees were significantly engaged with their employers in 2015. (Adkins, 2015)

Employee engagement is a buzzword, but it remains elusive to many companies today.

Clearly Arthur T. Demoulas is an exceptional leader. And, he will tell you that the key to his success has been to *focus on people.* His view is that if you treat people well, they will work harder for you: "If everyone in the workplace is equal and treated with dignity, they work with a little extra passion, a little extra dedication. I think that's a wonderful business message to the world." (Ross, 2014)

I believe the success of Market Basket is due to its treatment of people from the top leadership down. This is an essential part of the company's overall strategy. When Arthur says that everyone is equal and should be treated with dignity, his policies of paying good wages, helping employees through personal situations, showing loyalty to suppliers, and keeping prices affordable for customers all reinforce the strategy. What makes him an amazing leader and his company so successful is *the execution of that strategy every day*, the "How."

> **Disengaged employees typically care less about executing new efforts.**

Next we will look at examples in which leadership actions are *inconsistent* with strategies. The consequences, as you might imagine, are not good.

Leadership Inconsistency

Have you ever heard a leader tell you how important employees are to the success of the company and then watch the company cut a significant number of jobs? Or have you been told you were essential to the team and then never received a good raise or promotion? These are examples of inconsistency between strategy and leadership.

If a company has a strategy that emphasizes the importance of employees, then they should treat employees respectfully, with loyalty, and offer fair wage increases. If there is a disconnect between what leaders say and what the company does, employees will be less engaged and not very loyal. And, disengaged employees typically care less about executing new efforts.

Unfortunately, many examples exist of companies that have spent enormous amounts of time and money crafting brilliant strategies only to execute in a fashion that is inconsistent. Ultimately, the strategies fail.

I've been part of organizations that continuously stated the equal value of employees and shareholders, yet they repeatedly sacrificed loyal employees for the sake of short-term quarterly profit goals set arbitrarily for shareholders. In these situations, the *strategy* is right; people are indeed critical to the success of a business. But when a company doesn't treat the employees in a way that is consistent with their stated strategy, the result is high employee turnover and unenthusiastic employees. High turnover and disengaged employees are tough factors to overcome when you are trying to motivate people to adopt new ways of doing things.

All too often executives fail to recognize that an inconsistent leadership approach is the root of the problem, not the employees. A specific example of such inconsistency, in my view, was exhibited by the CEO of Yahoo, Marissa Mayer. Marissa took over as CEO for Yahoo in 2012. During her tenure, she made several unpopular decisions, such as removing the ability to work remotely in a company where a large percentage of employees used to have that flexibility.

The next key element for ensuring execution is understanding and meeting customer expectations.

Then in 2015, Marissa was pregnant with twins when she announced that she planned to take only two weeks' maternity leave. In the past, Yahoo had officially touted flexible benefit policies for employees. But now Marissa's actions conveyed that employees should be back at work quickly after the birth of a child. This is an example of a fatal flaw in execution. The policies supported the strategy, but the actions of leaders were inconsistent.

Therefore, what is critical to successful development and deployment of the "How" is not just the right strategy and policies, but also leadership actions that are consistent with the strategy.

Meeting Customer Expectations

The next key element for ensuring execution is understanding and meeting customer expectations. If you don't carefully consider how to meet customer expectations as you develop the strategy and execution plan, the outcome can be devastating to a company, as we will see in our next example.

Have you ever switched your provider for a service or product because they made a change that failed to meet your needs and expectations? Most likely, your provider did not do enough due diligence to assess the impact of the change on customers like yourself, or they may have decided to get out of that business for whatever reason. Whatever the case, you and many others probably switched to a different company.

We discussed the example of Netflix in the first chapter. But let's look at it again from the angle of meeting customer needs. Netflix is a company that made a huge change to their service without consulting customer. This occurred when Netflix entered the video streaming market. I'm a fan of Netflix, but it amazed me how they could make such a big misstep.

Remember that Netflix launched its "Qwikster" brand briefly in 2011 as a spinoff of their legacy DVD rental business. Video streaming was clearly the future at the time, as Reed Hastings, the famed CEO of Netflix, believed so correctly. His goal was to split his company and allow Netflix to focus on the development of the streaming business, which was the right strategy. But due to many leadership changes at Netflix at the time, Hastings made the decision quickly to spin off the DVD business. In so doing, he underestimated the customer backlash that would result from the 60 percent price increase that was required to maintain access to both services.

A company's culture must support a strategy for effective execution.

Moreover, customers had the added complexity of dealing with the two companies.

Netflix also did a poor job of communicating the changes to its customers. The execution was so flawed that it cost Netflix a loss of eight hundred thousand subscribers, a 77 percent stock-price drop in just four months, and a battered management reputation.

The story is a great case study on the importance of effective execution and how a failure to listen to your customers can be devastating. For this reason, Lean and Six Sigma methodologies always start with a focus on customer requirements. Developing a plan of execution with no input from your customers will likely end with the same results as Qwikster (Sandoval, 2012).

Company Culture

In addition to leadership and customer expectations, a company's culture must support a strategy for effective execution.

Think about your ideal company culture. What does it look like to you? Hopefully your ideal is similar to the company you work for, otherwise you might want to consider a career change. Cultures can vary significantly from company to company and industry to industry. Cultures vary *because they are tied to leadership*, the people who set the tone for how people function in the organization. If a company's culture is inconsistent with its strategy, it will likely struggle to be as successful as its potential.

When it comes to culture, few companies have figured it out as well as Google. They have enviously made it to the top spot on Fortune's Top 100 companies to work for an amazing seven times through 2016. Google made their business all around their people.

I like to say that business in general is all about people. People work for people and people buy from people. At Google, this is supported in a work environment, where leaders invest heavily in ongoing office atmosphere improvements for comfort and to inspire creativity. They strive to maintain an open culture and are always encouraging employees to try new ideas. They create places that are conducive to people meeting each other, which allows for brainstorming new ideas and increasing overall productivity. They include benefits such as onsite workout areas, childcare and laundry facilities to help the team with daily life functions.

All of these amazing benefits clearly support the "How," thereby reinforcing the value of people. The results have been amazing. Google is not only an amazing place to work, the company has achieved all this while recording a whopping $18 billion in net income in 2016. Their strategy is not unique, especially in the tech world, but they are clearly leading the pack in results.

On the other side of the spectrum is Sears, a company that, according to Glassdoor rankings, is one of the worst companies to work for. Sears has very low customer and employee satisfaction levels. Employees complain about unrealistic sales goals, which is related to the low number of customers. Overall, the holding company has reported over $1 billion in losses annually since 2014. The company strategy appears to offer more value and low prices, very similar to Market Basket, but Sears is failing miserably at execution. In a case like Sears, implementing change will be tough because employees are extremely dissatisfied and the company culture is lackluster.

Therefore, the health and consistency of a company's culture matters. It must support the strategy for the "How" to be effective.

In these examples, we can see the importance of the "How." The key elements to ensure execution include effective leadership, customer satisfaction, and the right company culture.

Assuming these are in place and execution is a success, your job as a leader or manager is still not done. The next critical component, outlined in more detail in the final chapter, is to monitor the business. This step requires the development of key measures of success, a method for measurement, and a plan of action based on analysis. Chapter 7 reviews several options to ensure successful execution, and the tools to identify future improvement efforts.

Rigorous measurement allows

executives to identify backsliding,

correct course where needed, and

demonstrate tangible evidence of improvement—

which can help to maintain positive momentum

over the long haul.

— KatzenbachIlona, Steffen & Kronley
Cultural Change That Sticks

CHAPTER 7

Monitoring for Success

re there any components of your job that are never measured? Imagine that a manager asks you to take extra steps to make life easier for another department, but you never get credit for taking those steps because they are not recorded. Or perhaps the manager who asked you to do this work decides to leave, which means that you're unsure if you should proceed with his or her directions. These situations occur because companies fail to monitor the execution of a strategy.

Therefore, once you have carefully deployed your change effort, the last—and perhaps most important—step in your journey will be to monitor results. Doing so will ensure consistent execution and adoption of the change by employees and customers.

Google constantly monitors and evaluates its business and people. Monitoring is part of its culture, and the company has clearly proven that it works. Much of Toyota's success over the years can also be attributed to a simple strategy, one that focuses on quality and continuous monitoring and improvement efforts.

If having a simple strategy and monitoring it closely works so well, then why don't more companies do it? As the title of this chapter suggests, monitoring is simple, not easy. Based on my experience, most companies monitor results in some fashion, but they may not be measuring and controlling the right items. They may be tracking too many metrics, or their motives for change might have nothing to do with past results.

We will examine the first two reasons in this chapter, within the context of Six Sigma's control phase and the concept of Key Performance Indicators.

First, companies often do not measure the right items because they don't leverage a good process for doing so. We are going to take a high-level look at how to leverage Six Sigma's Control phase tool to ensure you are looking at the right elements, have a plan to track consistently, and adjust if necessary when results are not meeting expectations. Monitoring results does not need to be complicated, and one does not need to be an expert in statistics to keep track of progress.

Companies often do not measure the right items because they don't leverage a good process for doing so.

To keep it simple, we will focus on the elements within the Six Sigma Control plan detailed on the next page. For your reference, I've created the sample on the next page with several process steps or areas to be monitored. You can find many other examples online depending on what you are trying to monitor. Essentially, you create a control plan to monitor a process and then you list each of your process steps. We will walk through each item on the sample control plan on the next page.

Control Plan Components

1. **Process Name:** This refers to the process or initiative you are trying to monitor. Examples might be "Customer Wait Time" or "Product Quality Improvement."

2. **Process Owner:** This is the person responsible for the process. It could be the individual creating the control plan, but that is not always the case.

3. **Business:** This should describe the business that the process is found in.

4. **Preparer:** This is the individual creating the control plan.

5. **Owner Email:** Include the process owner's email for contact purposes.

6. **Date Created:** Use the initial date the control plan was created.

7. **Date Update:** The last date the control plan was updated.

Control Plan: sample

Process Name: _____ Owner Email: _____ Date Created: _____

Process Owner: _____ Date Updated: _____

Business: _____ Approval: _____

Preparer: _____

Process Step	Process Step Input(s)	Process Step Output(s)	Process Step Owner	Process Performance Characteristics				Control Methods					
				Lower Spec Limit	Upper Spec Limit	Target	Customer CTQ	Out of Control Conditions	Measurement System for Process — Evaluation	Sample — Size	Sample — Frequency	Method for Observation	Reaction Plan
Customer Checks in Hotel	Customer Arrives at Hotel	Customer Goes to Room	Front Desk Attendant	0 wait time	5 minutes wait time	>3 Min	<1 min	large groups arriving at same time; new employees still in training; many employees call out sick	Internal data capture	All	Daily	Inspection	Review staffing and room utilization for all days out of control to make future adjustments as needed.
Sales Performance Indicators Report refresh	Updated monthly data available	Distribute report to key business leaders	Report Manager	97% Accuracy	100% accuracy	100% accuracy	100% accuracy	Organizational changes impacting input data; data quality issues with external data supplier	Manual	5	per report	Inspection	Review report timing and adjust if possible

8. **Approval:** You should include individuals or business that have approved the plan as needed.

9. **Process Step:** This is the specific step in the process are you monitoring.

10. **Process Input:** This is the input to the process step you are monitoring. See the examples above, essentially, and think about what needs to happen just before your step.

11. **Process Output:** This is the output of the step you are monitoring. For example, if you are ensuring that a wait time is within an acceptable range, the output would be the completion of whatever it is the customer was waiting for, such as a completed check-out, a package shipped, a report sent, etc.

12. **Process Step Owner:** This is the person who is ultimately responsible for a specific process. In larger companies or projects, you might have multiple process owners listed within a control plan.

13. **Process Performance Characteristics:** This section outlines how you expect the process to perform and what your customer expects. For Six Sigma, the process requirements always start with customer expectations, regardless of whether a business is prepared to meet them.

14. **Lower and Upper Spec Limits:** Within Six Sigma, there are statistical methods to quantify lower and upper specification limits that are not the same as customer requirements. Although we are not going to cover the statistical calculations here, ideally limits are based on the measurable variation within a process and not on arbitrary limits set by a business. In the absence of statistical process control limits, business specifications set by leadership are better than having no requirements at all to measure performance. In the example given for wait times, management may have customer feedback that suggests they will not change providers unless the wait time consistently exceeds five minutes, and, therefore, management sets the upper limit of wait time to five minutes.

15. Target: This is the desired goal for the process step. Typically, the target equals the customer requirement, although it may not be feasible to achieve the customer's expectation 100 percent of the time. For example, in the wait time example, the customer may expect zero wait-time. It is very difficult to provide staff that could provide zero wait-time in a business where demand is not predictable. Therefore, the business has set a target of a three-minute wait, knowing that customers will likely not move their business elsewhere until the wait time exceeds five minutes.

16. Customer CTQ: CTQ stands for "Critical to Quality and Customer." CTQ defines what is critical to the customer in terms of your product or service. Gathering input on what is important to your customer is often referred to as Voice of Customer or VOC. You can gather feedback many ways including surveys, focus groups, in person, etc. Determining CTQs occurs by taking customer comments or quotes and translating them into issues and specifications. Those specifications become the CTQ and must be met to satisfy the customer requirement.

17. Control Methods: This is the category for identifying an out-of-control condition, the measurement system, the types of samples that will be taken (in terms of size or number of samples, and the frequency), and method for observation. For example, in the hotel check-in process, various factors could cause the wait time to exceed the upper specification limit of five minutes, such as unexpected large groups arriving, new employees in training, or many employees calling in sick at the same time. The control plan identifies what the issues are and then what will be done to fix them. Some companies have systems to capture critical measures such as wait time, quality, errors, etc. If data is collected automatically, time reports are often able to reflect 100 percent of the sample. Frequency simply means how often samples are taken. This could be hourly, daily, weekly, monthly, etc. Finally, the method for observation refers to how issues will be identified.

18. Reaction Plan: This outlines what will be done to rectify processes that don't meet expectations. In the example above, the hotel could add a staffing alert for when large groups are booked at the hotel so that staff could be added or so that the process could be streamlined to avoid long wait times. This is exactly why hotels will often check-in groups prior to arrival.

Engage Key Stakeholders

Lastly, as you create a control plan, you will need to engage your key stakeholders because they will be responsible for various components and corrective actions. There are many other tools within Six Sigma that can be leveraged to monitor a process, and there are great resources available to help you, if needed. Whatever tools you choose, the key is to use them consistently to ensure the process has been fixed and to potentially identify further enhancements.

Whatever tools you choose, the key is to use them consistently to ensure the process has been fixed and to potentially identify further enhancements.

While the Six Sigma control phase tends to be most useful upon the completion of a project, all businesses I've been a part of had some type of scorecard or key measures they used to measure the success of the business. A familiar term for referring to these types of measures is Key Performance Indicators, or KPIs.

Key Performance Indicators (KPIs)

Some companies have so many KPIs that no one is sure which measures to focus on or what they all mean. Although many companies have KPIs, they may not be the right ones, or in some cases there are way too many.

Nevertheless, KPIs can be incredibly useful to a business, depending on how they are developed and leveraged. To be effective, KPIs must align to the overall mission and strategy of a business. Typically, KPIs focus on four main areas.

Revenue Improvement: All for profit companies need to measure financial factors such as net profit, gross margin, actual vs. projected revenue, sales, and cost of goods sold.

People: Several key measures for managing people include employee satisfaction, turnover rate, and engagement.

Process Cycle-Time Improvement: Examples include product quality measures such as percent of defects, customer support tickets, time to fulfill orders, etc.

Customer Satisfaction: Measuring information about customers can be done by looking at overall customer satisfaction, retention, and cost of acquisition.

The right mix of KPIs varies depending on the strategy of the business. For a high-end retailer, such as Nordstrom, the primary measure is likely to be overall customer satisfaction. Cost containment is less important. Another low-cost provider, such as Walmart, is going to focus more on keeping the cost of goods low and having good efficiency measures since the profit margins are low.

To be effective, KPIs must align to the overall mission and strategy of a business.

Another important point is to keep the critical list of KPIs limited to five to ten. It's essential that employees can understand the most important measures aligned to a strategy to help ensure goals are met. I've been a part of many businesses with so many measures that employees felt deflated when they couldn't achieve them all. Smart leaders pick the critical few metrics that align to their strategy and that are measurable. The next page shows a sample chart with five KPIs for the first quarter.

As we see, most businesses have a mix of measures they monitor with a specific goal. In this case, we see that customer satisfaction has been consistently below 95 percent of the goal, while the percentage of products with defects has been above the goal. Likely these two measures are correlated, but additional analysis would be needed to validate such a conclusion.

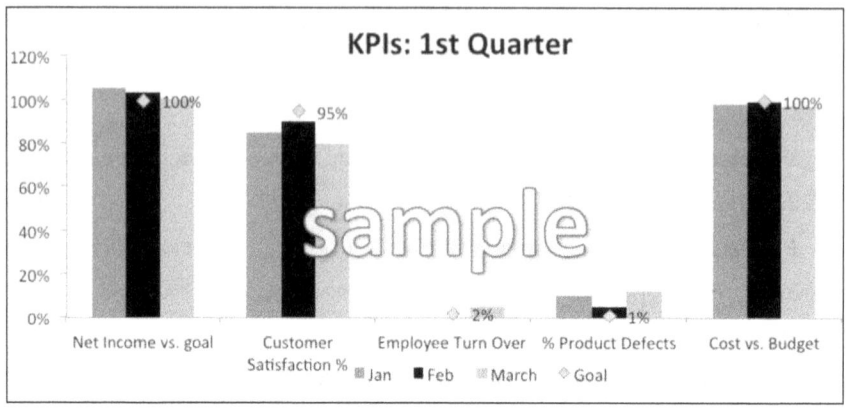

Smaller businesses tend to monitor fewer measures. Those are typically total sales or net revenue, due to limited resources or expertise. Sales revenue is obviously important, but it's what I'd call a "rearview mirror" measure because it only indicates what has already happened versus what is going to happen. Businesses need to also have forward looking measures, such as a sales pipeline, to ensure enough new revenue will be coming in to achieve forecasts. Other critical measures include customer satisfaction, employee satisfaction, and quality measures.

Lastly, much has already been written about the need for KPIs and how to develop the right ones based on the business strategy. I'd suggest that many businesses still fall short, whether they are large companies that over-measure, or small companies that tend to under-measure. Smart companies that focus on execution have likely identified the critical few measures that will account for most of their success (applying the 80/20 rule) and they monitor them closely. By applying this simple approach, they will be able to monitor and achieve success.

Smart companies that focus on execution have likely identified the critical few measures that will account for most of their success (applying the 80/20 rule) and they monitor them closely.

Whether a company uses Six Sigma methodologies, KPIs, or some other type of scorecard approach is less relevant than the fact that a company is using some type of method to monitor the success of the business. Although this sounds like common sense, many businesses get into trouble by not monitoring effectiveness. I believe monitoring doesn't happen as often as it should because leaders get busy and because monitoring is not as exciting as developing the next best idea. That's true for the "How" in general, of which monitoring is a key element of success.

Conclusion

No matter what size business you are a part of, or what your role is, hopefully this book has provided a fresh and comprehensive look at the importance of elevating the "How" when you are developing or executing the next brilliant strategy. I also hope it has provided you with practical tools and ideas to ensure success.

Remember the components of a successful implementation include: quickly determining the right strategy, developing a P.L.A.N. for execution, leveraging proven tools, the critical importance of leadership support, effective communications, and monitoring for success.

By mastering these concepts you will become a more valuable employee able to respectfully push back on leaders to ensure they have a P.L.A.N. for execution, and if they don't, you will know how to develop one! Or, you will be the leader that ensures the organization focuses more on the "How" than the "What." Regardless of your role, you will agree that in the end, *It's all about the "How."*

How to Handle
the Next "Best" Idea

So, you have just finished reading this book and you are alerted to a new urgent email announcing a mandatory all-staff conference call later in the day. I typically dreaded those calls, since they often meant significant changes were on the horizon for me, my staff, or both.

What do you do? If you are an employee receiving the news that your world is about to change, I encourage you to boldly and respectfully examine the effort to ensure due diligence has been done to get to the root of problem, that communications are clear, that leadership and employees are engaged, and that the change is aligned with the official company strategy. If any of these components are missing, you should display your leadership skills by asking questions and offering solutions. Pretty much anyone can identify problems, but leaders also offer solutions.

If you are a leader or manager, consider if your strategy *really* needs to be changed, or if the problem is with the *execution*. Resist the urge to change for the sake of change. Ask your trusted and experienced advisors, as well as customers, to further evaluate if changing your strategy is needed. Use the tools in this book to determine the root of lackluster results.

If the strategy must be changed, remember that doing so will be a challenge and to leverage a thorough approach such as the DMAIC process in Six Sigma to engage the right stakeholders and outline a project charter.

Then define your business case and determine a timeline to improve results. Gather data to help determine the best course of action and then pause to analyze. Once you are fully powered with information, craft your plan for improvement and identify the metrics you will need to monitor and control the changes on an ongoing basis.

Sadly, I've observed brilliant strategies get retooled just because of leadership changes or Wall Street pressure to produce unrealistic double-digit quarterly profits. I once worked for a remarkable leader who inherently loved change. We were constantly developing and executing new models. Although that business was generally successful, the company expended unnecessary amounts of brainpower and money to continuously reinvent itself for relatively little return.

In general, I'd estimate that these types of unnecessary changes cost US companies billions of dollars every year in endless hours spent in planning meetings, reorganizing, developing communication materials, changing technology, training employees, creating new tools, etc. I should know, since for several years my paycheck was based primarily on successfully leading change efforts.

Often, new initiatives are not given enough time to be successful or to be rolled out properly. So remember, patience is a fruit of the spirit, and decent strategies, when given the right amount of time to be implemented (the "How"), will produce lastly results, saving companies time and money.

References

Adkins, A. (2015, March). U.S. Employee Engagement Reaches Three-Year High. *http://www.gallup.com/poll/181895/employee-engagement-reaches-three-year-high.aspx.*

Carmody, B. (2015, August). Why 96 Percent of Businesses Fail Within 10 Years. *http://www.inc.com/bill-carmody/why-96-of-businesses-fail-within-10-years.html.*

Chapman, G. and White, P. (2012). *The 5 Languages of Appreciation in the Workplace.* Empowering Organizations by Encouraging People. Revised and Updated. Northfield Publishing. (Pages 15, 46, 59, 73, 93-102).

Deloitte LLP CFO Survey, *Strategy and Growth Decisions and Major Change Initiatives Add to CFOs' Career Stresses, http://deloitte.wsj.com/cfo/2012/10/24/strategy-and-growth-decisions-and-major-change-initiatives-add-to-cfos-career-stresses/?KEYWORDS=define+business+strategy, October 2012.*

Drucker, P. (1963, May). Managing for Business Effectiveness. Harvard Business Review. *https://hbr.org/1963/05/managing-for-business-effectiveness.*

Katzenbach, J. R., Steffen, I., Kronley, C. (2012, August). Cultural Change That Sticks. Harvard Business Review. *https://hbr.org/2012/07/cultural-change-that-sticks.*

Keyte, C. (2012, October). 90% of Business Strategies Fail Due to Poor Execution, *http://www.business2community.com/strategy/90-of-business-strategies-fail-due-to-poor-execution-0319429.*

Korschun, D. and Welker, G. (2015). *We Are Market Basket: The Story of the Unlikely Grassroots Movement that Saved a Beloved Business.* AMACOM.

Lafley, A.G. & Martin, R.L. (2013). *Playing to Win.* Harvard Business Review Press. (Page 141).

McChesney, C., Covey, S., Huling, J. (2012) *The 4 Disciplines of Execution: Achieving Your Wildly Important Goals.* Reprint Edition. Free Press. (Page 23).

Power, B. How Toyota Pulls Improvement from the Front Line. *https://hbr.org/2011/06/how-toyota-pulls-improvement-f/*, June 2011.

Ross, C. Arthur T. Demoulas Happy 'just being a grocer.' *https://www.bostonglobe.com/business/2014/09/11/after-epic-market-basket-battle-arthur-demoulas-happy-just-being-grocer/Iqd3AyAX6qh36fhldPOyPN/story.html*, September 2014.

Sandoval, G. (2012, July). Netflix's lost year: The inside story of the price-hike train wreck. *http://www.cnet.com/news/netflixs-lost-year-the-inside-story-of-the-price-hike-train-wreck/*.

Stettinius, W., Wood, D. R. Jr., Doyle, J. L. and Colley, J. L. (2005). *How to Plan and Execute Strategy.* First Edition. McGraw-Hill Education. (Page 89).

Weiner, J. (2014, April). Just Because You Said it, Doesn't Make it So. *https://www.linkedin.com/pulse/20140428141014-22330283-just-because-you-said-it-doesn-t-make-it-so*.

Welch, J. (2005). *Winning.* First Edition. HarperCollins Publishing. (Page 166).